Much has been written about the next generation leaving the church. Not enough has been done to help us see why they stay. Parr and Crites help masterfully here. What they learned from their study is both useful and encouraging.

Dr. Alvin L. Reid
Professor of Evangelism & Student Ministry,
Southeastern Baptist Theological Seminary,
Wake Forest, North Carolina

As the parent of three adult children who are vibrant Christians, who "stayed" with their faith when they transitioned from living at home to college years and then full independence–this book excites me! Rather than analyzing those who left, these researchers have answered the question "what works?" and summarized their insights for us. Parents–read this book as a prescription for future parenting practices. As you focus on the positive factors that lead to life-long faithfulness, you can have confidence you are doing your best to give your children the opportunity to remain faithful to the Lord throughout their lifetime.

Dr. Jeff Iorg
President, Golden Gate Baptist Theological Seminary,
Mill Valley, California

For the last decade or so, youth ministry and youth ministers have been getting a little beat up with the statistics that seem to indicate that teenagers who were active in youth ministry are bailing out of the church as young adults. Some of the conclusions reached have been valid and some have been illogical and far-reaching.

I have the privilege of standing in front of young adults who are preparing for a lifetime of ministry in church, church planting, or the mission field. They did not drop out of church or the faith. I applaud the research effort by my friend Steve Parr and his friend Tom Crites which investigates why others stay engaged in faith communities.

Why They Stray

Helping Parents and Church Leaders Make Investments
That Keep Children and Teens Connected to the
Church for a Lifetime

Dr. Steve R. Parr and Dr. Tom Crites

WESTBOW
PRESS®
A DIVISION OF THOMAS NELSON
& ZONDERVAN

Scripture taken from the New King James Version. Copyright © 1979, 1980, 1982 by Thomas Nelson, Inc. Used by permission. All rights reserved.

Scripture taken from the Holman Christian Standard Bible ® Copyright © 2003, 2002, 2000, 1999 by Holman Bible Publishers. All rights reserved.

Scripture taken from the Holy Bible, NEW INTERNATIONAL VERSION®. Copyright © 1973, 1978, 1984, 2011 by Biblica, Inc. All rights reserved worldwide. Used by permission. NEW INTERNATIONAL VERSION® and NIV® are registered trademarks of Biblica, Inc. Use of either trademark for the offering of goods or services requires the prior written consent of Biblica US, Inc.

WestBow Press books may be ordered through booksellers or by contacting:

WestBow Press
A Division of Thomas Nelson & Zondervan
1663 Liberty Drive
Bloomington, IN 47403
www.westbowpress.com
1 (866) 928-1240

ISBN: 978-1-5127-0882-0 (sc)
ISBN: 978-1-5127-0883-7 (hc)
ISBN: 978-1-5127-0881-3 (e)

Library of Congress Control Number: 2015913452

Print information available on the last page.

WestBow Press rev. date: 08/27/2015

Dedicated in appreciation to my parents
Ben and Betty Parr
And
In memory of my grandparents
Quinton and Wilma Warbington Rooks
Adolphus and Ila Harrison Parr
From Steve R. Parr

Dedicated to my parents
Larry Crites, Judy Tucker and Rex Tucker
My wife, Cyndy
And to my kids
Kaylynn and Brice who I hope will always Stay
From Tom Crites

CONTENTS

FOREWORD

As a professor of evangelism and student ministry, I'm often asked to speak on issues related to reaching and keeping the next generation. The American church is not doing a phenomenal job of either at the moment. In my tradition, the Southern Baptist Convention, a recent report noted that 80% of the 45,000 churches in the SBC had seen 0-1 young adults baptized from the ages of eighteen to twenty-nine in an entire year.

A statistic like that makes me wonder whether churches are putting up signs out front that read: "You are not welcome here," to that demographic. Further, the largest study of youth and religion in U.S. history—the National Institute of Youth and Religion—determined that the overall content in the teaching of most churches aimed at youth is Moralistic Therapeutic Deism. It's primarily about morality, teaching youth right from wrong. It's therapeutic—that is, it's aimed at making youth feel good about themselves—and it worships a God who made the world but who is not directly involved in their lives.

I saw this demonstrated when speaking at a missions conference in a college town some time back. A young lady in her mid-20s came to me after I spoke on principles for reaching the next generation. She told me she had grown up in church and was active in her youth group, but she left church in college and only recently had genuinely been changed by the gospel. She told me when she reflected on her youth ministry days, the two things she remembered most were these two statements: "Don't have sex," and "Invite a friend." Not a lot about Jesus. Not a focus on relationships or the family. Not a unified vision for discipleship—just behavior modification.

I've run into that mindset a lot over the last few years. What are we really trying to do with the next generation? Get them in our church buildings? Or build Christ in them? Are they so different, so unlike those who went before them in churches that we are simply incapable of reaching them, or of even keeping those who have grown up in church?

This is where this book by my friends Steve Parr and Tom Crites can help. "Facts..." Ed Stetzer (President of LifeWay Research) has noted, "...are our friends." It's an easy thing to panic over changing times or to fret over the spirituality of a given generation. It's another to analyze what is really happening both for the negative and the positive trends.

Much has been written about the next generation leaving the church. Not enough has been done to help us see why they stay. Parr and Crites help masterfully here. What they learned from their study is both useful and encouraging. The reasons young people stayed in church and thus the ways to help keep youth in church are not seated in some new jargon or platform beyond the reach of a typical pastor or traditional church. Keeping the next generation does not require an unusual level of cultural savvy, but it does require a confidence in God's Word, the gospel, and in relationships. The things that matter—family, conversion, church engagement, key spiritual leaders—are rooted in the very way God wired us. In other words, rather than calling the church to jettison everything she has done and learn some new digital-age approach, Parr and Crites demonstrate how healthy families (biological families and the local church) make a remarkable difference in keeping young people in church. As you read this, see what your church is already doing. Locate areas where you can change. And, as the Psalmist said, we can see the next generation follow the Lord:

> *"He established a testimony in Jacob*
> *and set up a law in Israel,*
> *which He commanded our fathers*
> *to teach to their children*
> *So that a future generation —*
> *children yet to be born — might know.*

They were to rise and tell their children
so that they might put their confidence in God
and not forget God's works,
but keep His commands." (Psalm 78:5–7 HCSB)

Alvin L. Reid, Professor of Evangelism and Student Ministry/ Bailey Smith Chair of Evangelism, Southeastern Baptist Theological Seminary, Wake Forest, NC

INTRODUCTION

The church in North America is eroding. The number of people who claim to have a faith relationship with Jesus Christ decreases dramatically with each existing generation. The senior adults living today are the most saved generation alive, but as you survey the Baby Boomers and the generations that follow, the numbers decline. This is impacting churches in North America. We are going to share the data with you and will reveal how attendance in Christian churches is decreasing.

However, we are not pessimists. We are going to look at the cold hard facts, but we want to share a message that gives you hope and shows you where to place your efforts to make a difference. Allow us to give you a little background and a quick preview of what you will discover in this book. Here are a few things that we believe will give you context and help you to know our hearts as authors:

1. We have a faith relationship with the Lord Jesus Christ and seek daily to serve and to grow in intimacy with Him.
2. We believe the Bible is the inspired Word of God and is totally trustworthy.
3. We believe the Lord Jesus Christ established the church, and it will never die.
4. We believe that the North American church is in need of an awakening, and that it will not come up from man but must come down from God.

5. We believe that we have a responsibility to share the gospel and to invite people to come into a faith relationship with Jesus Christ.
6. We believe that we are to serve and invest in local churches to encourage them to be healthy and thriving in ministering to their congregations and reaching out to their communities.

Certainly that is not all that we believe, but this serves as a context for who we are and what our convictions are. We believe in evangelism and are convinced that we must do all that we can to reach the next generation. We want you to hear that, but this is not a book about reaching the next generation. It is actually more of a book about reaching the generation that is yet to be born. The 78th Psalm speaks of our generational responsibility and speaks of sharing the story of God's deliverance so that those who have yet to be born may know it. We believe that if we are not effective at keeping the young people we have in our churches right now connected and growing, there will not be anyone to reach the future generations in North America.

Much has been written about younger adults and their demise in church commitment. We will reference that to some degree, but we were determined to take a different approach that turned out to have powerful results. We have already begun to share the results, and the reception has been enthusiastic. Instead of asking why young adults are leaving the church, we surveyed those who grew up in church, are still serving faithfully in the church, and studied "why they stay." We surveyed young adults, ages twenty-six through thirty-nine. The only other criterion was that they grew up going to church. It was a national survey, and the results were revealing. You will learn as a pastor, parent, or church leader specific actions that you can take to make a definitive difference in whether or not the fifteen-year-olds attending your church now are still attending and serving when they turn thirty.

Is that not what is supposed to be happening? When we "make disciples" as we are commanded in the Great Commission, is it not our aim that they would continue to grow and serve, not only for a season, but for a lifetime? We discovered fifteen major issues, fourteen of which can be addressed directly by your congregation to enhance the discipleship of your younger members. You are going to be encouraged and challenged, and you will find tangible actions that you can take. Please get this book into the hands of as many parents as possible. We discovered huge implications for the way we raise our children as Christian parents. Also, share it with your pastor and church leaders. The time is now and the time is short, not only to reach the next generation, but also to take actions that connect the younger members of our church now for a lifetime of discipleship so that they can reach a generation that is yet to be born.

We know that many of the younger generation have strayed. Many have stopped attending church. We love the Lord. We love the church. We love children, students, and young adults. Join us on this journey as we learn something perhaps more important...for those who have not left the church...why they stay!

PART ONE
WON'T YOU STAY?

CHAPTER ONE

DEATH OF A CONGREGATION

Steve Parr

The church of the Lord Jesus Christ will never die. However, a congregation can and sometimes does. The Lord is adding to the church daily those who are being saved. That has been happening since the Day of Pentecost, and there are more Christians living today than at any time in the history of the world. However, in North America, fewer people are coming to faith in Christ and the number of church attendees is eroding. Some churches are closing their doors. If these were rural churches in sparsely populated areas or places where economic circumstances have resulted in a severe population decline, you might argue that the issue is more of a demographic dilemma.

I live in a county with a population of 860,000. It is a suburban area that stretches twenty to fifty miles outside of a major city. The county was listed as one of the fastest growing in the United States just over a decade ago. I have heard several pastors proclaim that "anybody could grow a congregation if they pastored in that county." Yet, living here I am well aware of congregations that have not grown in the past thirty or more years.

I was shocked last year when two local churches located within ten miles of my home closed their doors. These were not rural, struggling, small, divided congregations. Both averaged more than 200 in attendance within the past twenty years. How can that happen? How can a congregation die when it is located within the reach of not just hundreds but thousands of people?

Recently, I was invited to consult with a church. The pastor was concerned about the fact that no one was being reached. He shared that the congregation averaged about twenty in worship each Sunday. I arrived on a Wednesday night to provide consultation, insight, and recommendations for improving outreach. I knew the church was in deep trouble as soon as I laid eyes on the congregation.

You must understand that they were not in trouble because of the number of people present. They were a small congregation that averaged twenty, and frankly that was not the problem. The Bible never prescribes the size of a congregation. A congregation can be healthy with twenty members, 200 members, or 2,000 members. It was a small church and there is nothing wrong with that. It is not the size of the church that matters but rather the size of God that makes the difference. God does big things through small congregations. The problem was that just a couple of short years prior to my visit, they were averaging over forty. In other words, it was not the size of the congregation that was the concern, but rather the erosion of the congregation was the issue. They will be closing the doors soon if the decline is not reversed. How did they get into this position?

One of my first observations was the age of the seventeen members who showed up to meet with me on that Wednesday evening. I am fifty-five years of age, and on this evening I would have comprised the youth group! With visions of lock-ins in my head I noted that only one person was in my age grouping and most were easily a decade or more older than me. I love senior adults, and I am quickly closing in on membership in that life stage. However, a congregation comprised of only empty-nesters, grandparents, and retirees is in serious trouble. I had some questions.

Following some introductory remarks I conducted a brief, informal survey. "How many of you work with the preschool ministry?" I asked to begin the consultation. How many hands do you think were raised? You are correct if you guessed that none went up. "Who among you serve as leaders in the children's ministry?" I asked. You guessed it. No hands were raised. "Who has responsibility for ministering to the students?" I continued. I was on a roll and I knew the answer before I asked the questions, but I had a point to make.

"I imagine you think that you need no preschool leaders because you have no preschoolers attending," I pointed out. "However, you likely have no preschoolers attending because you have no preschool leadership. No one has responsibility for ministering and reaching out to families with babies, toddlers, and kindergarteners."

When was it that this church decided to no longer reach out to younger people? I don't imagine they ever had a business meeting where someone made a motion saying, "Brother moderator, I move that our church cease from loving, caring for, providing for, or reaching out to any parent of a child under the age of six, and further recommend that we close our nursery and preschool area." No such motion was ever made and no second to the motion was ever offered. Yet they are in the same position at this point as if the motion had literally been made, and further, as if the congregation gave unanimous consent.

I added another question to drive home my point. "Tell me about your forthcoming plans for Vacation Bible School," I continued. "We are not having VBS this year," was the reply. The church conducted the summer outreach ministry for children annually for much of their history, so why have they discontinued it? Once again they might justify the reason as to why they conduct no Vacation Bible School with the fact that they have no children attending. The reality is that the fewer children a congregation has, the more important an outreach ministry for children and families like Vacation Bible School is. They need to engage in such a ministry, not because they have children attending, but because they do not. With acknowledgement that VBS is not essential to have a healthy church, it is still an effective and credible method of reaching children and families. This congregation made the mistake of thinking that it was a ministry for *their* children instead of an outreach to children and families in the community, as it is actually intended to be.

Even the smallest church needs to have someone responsible for focusing on the leadership of preschool-age boys and girls, along with reaching out to the parents of this age group. When a congregation loves babies and toddlers, they love young adults in their twenties and early thirties. They must likewise have someone focused on children as well as a leader focused on students. The way you reach students in high school is not the same way you reach and minister

5

to adults who are empty-nesters. The energy and strategy required to reach teens must be purposeful and specific to their needs. At the point you cease providing leadership and purposefully reaching out to any of these life stages in particular: preschool, children, and students, you will in turn fail to reach and minister to young adults and you might as well make a formal motion in a business meeting to stop loving on young people. The result will be the same. The congregation is going to die. The death will not be immediate but will likely be slow, sad, and painful. I asked the congregation to envision driving up to the church one day to an empty parking lot and realizing that they could not enter the worship center because a padlock and chain had been placed on the front door. That is a tragic mental picture, but it is necessary because it represents the future of the congregation if something does not change.

The pastor reminded the congregation of a young lady who visited a few short weeks prior with her three children. She actually asked what the congregation had for the children and they pointed out that nothing was available for their age group. She stayed for their morning services, but would it surprise you to know that she never returned? Do you know what may be the most unsettling part of this story? No one knows if she ever tried to connect with another congregation or if she was even a believer. It is sobering to think that she may have been searching spiritually and the congregation was not prepared to meet her needs because they were not prepared for her children.

How can this happen? I want to give some benefit of the doubt to the congregation in this regard. I believe the members love the Lord. I believe they love their church. I believe they will go to heaven when they die. But will anyone stand up and say, "I won't let this congregation die on my watch!" It will take radical action to turn it around. They do have options, but all of them will be painful:

- They could merge with another congregation.
- They could allow a strong, healthy church to adopt them and give the sponsoring church full authority to make changes needed to survive.
- They could turn the church over to a church planter and be absorbed by the new congregation.

- They could invite a healthy church to send several families as missionaries for a year to give a leadership boost.
- They could move services to 8:30 a.m. and give the 11:00 a.m. hour to a church plant to share their facilities.

Please do not interpret any of these ideas to be outside of a powerful move of God upon the congregation. Indeed, God may simply do something miraculous, and understand that the members have been praying for their church. I got the sense when I finished that they did not like any of the solutions I offered. The pastor in essence said that they would just "try harder." If you always do what you have always done, you will always get what you have always got. The congregation is going to die.

No generation should be ignored. However, any congregation that fails to reach out to younger groups will eventually die. It is not easy. They think differently. They demand attention. They make lots of mistakes. They are immature. They are tough on the facilities. They don't give like we think they should. They sometimes misbehave. They have short attention spans. They are not as committed as we think they should be. In reality they are much like we were when we were young! You will be uncomfortable if your congregation commits to reach young adults, students, and children. Remember this: comfort is a great blessing, but it is never the mission. I fear that many congregations have made comfort the mission. The mission is the Great Commission. The motive is the Great Commandment. We are to love God with ALL of our hearts. We are to reach and minister to ALL nations, and that means all generations. A failure to do so will result in the death of a congregation.

QUESTIONS FOR DISCUSSION

1. How would you characterize the health of the following in your church: Preschool ministry? Children's ministry? Student ministry? Ministry to younger adults?
2. How does your congregation compare with your community in relation to different life stages that are present week to week?
3. Would you describe your congregation as thriving or struggling? If thriving, how might you help a struggling congregation? If struggling, is there a thriving congregation that you might connect with to make your congregation stronger in the future?

CHAPTER TWO

REALITY CHECK

Tom Crites

What is it about Starbucks? It seems that every young adult can tell you the precise location of the nearest Starbucks. They love to stop in and slap down five bucks for coffee and other coffee like drinks. They love to sit around and spend time soaking in the ambiance and posting pictures and comments of their coffee time via Instagram. I have to admit, I do not like Starbucks. The coffee is too expensive for me and does not really taste any better than my home brew. The atmosphere is intimidating for an older guy, with all the ordering lingo and exotic flavoring systems. I feel like I get this, "You just want a plain coffee?" look from the barista every time I go in there. But you cannot keep young adults out of the place. Can we agree that it would be nice if my church was a place where young adults loved to visit? It would be great if every church was a comfortable spot where young adults could enjoy each other's company and even take selfies. If the church was a place of refuge—where needs were met and questions were answered—wouldn't that be nice?

Unfortunately, in most churches young adults feel the way I feel at a Starbucks—out of place. As a result, church leaders have seen their congregation turn grey while millions of young people who claim to be Christians disconnect as they move from adolescence into early adulthood. In the past, young adults that transitioned from youth groups to "big church" went through a similar period of church

9

skipping. Young believers who actively participated in church life as teens interrupted their participation during their early twenties, but then returned to church life after they were married and when children came along. Current trends are pointing to the fact that young adults are not returning to church after their twenties. Leaders like Ken Ham are sounding an alarm: "Most youth of today will not be coming to church tomorrow . . . the next generation are calling it quits on the traditional church."[1]

George Barna's (an expert in the study of American religious beliefs and behaviors) research points out that only 20% of young adults who were active in church as teens were still active in church at the age of twenty-nine.[2] Moreover, there is a shrinking population of people who grew up in church, leading to fewer and fewer adults having church on their radar after transitioning from adolescence.[3] Current research shows that those returning often return at a lower level of commitment than before they strayed from the fold.[4] If one were to enter just about any traditional mainline church in America, he would quickly see a disproportionate number of gray-headed folks in comparison to all others.[5] Add it all up and you see this is a big problem.

Experts who study church dynamics have tried to understand the issue and have come up with a few worthy hypotheses. Some believe that this may be a conversion problem. Maybe those who *thought* they were Christians in their teen years did not experience a true conversion. The external motivation to attend and fellowship with other believers disappeared as they moved away from family and friends, and any intrinsic motivation to attend church was removed when the non-believer was released into the world. Thom Rainer, a leader in church health research, has been observing a devastating trend for several years that may point to the conversion problem. He tracked the unbelievers by generation and found that 35% of those born before 1946, the "Builder" generation, did not have a relationship with Jesus. The next generation, "Boomers," have about 65% of their population who are without Christ. He calls the children of the "Boomers," "Busters." These folks were born between 1965 and 1984, and 85% of them are unbelievers. The final group he identified, the "Bridger" generation, was estimated to have 96% non-Christians.[6] The only encouraging note is that more of this generation is inclined to come to faith since they are younger, but the numbers will still be staggering even if it increased by as much as 10%. It remains to be seen how faith will appear amongst our next generation, the "Millennials." If what Rainer has observed is true, then we have a lost population that does not see the spiritual benefit of attending church.

In addition to what Thom Rainer reported, David Kinnaman from Barna Research found that: "Teenagers are some of the most religiously active Americans . . . American twenty-somethings are the least religiously active."[7] He also stated: "Millions of young adults (Mosaics age 18-29) leave active involvement in church as they exit their teen years. Some never return, while others live indefinitely at the margins of the faith community, attempting to define their own spirituality."[8] Kay Powell and Chap Clark, authors of *Sticky Faith*, offer the observation that only 50% of Christian teens who were active in a church youth group "continue with their faith" into their college years.[9] Statistics like these may help validate the conversion problem, or they may point to another issue altogether.

Perhaps the consensus of thought in the paragraphs above points not to a conversion problem, but to a relevancy problem. Is it possible young adult Christians are feeling that the church is not relevant to their lives, or that their lives are not relevant to the church? In America today, only about 16% of all churches across every denomination have a significant young adult population.[10] It could be that something in the current environment has driven young Christians away from the church. If we were really honest with each other, we would have to admit that young adults are not seeing much of a difference in Christians and non-Christians in our culture today. Research indicates that this new wave of believers is not staying to fight for their place in church life; rather, they are moving on. They feel unfulfilled, isolated, judged, and dismissed. If young adults have to choose between their culture, their technology, their friends, and their church, more and more are not choosing their local church.

It could be that at the moment, there is something deeper occurring in this sociological phenomenon. Over ten years ago, there was a sense of optimism in the research: "Although some young believers are moving away from church, many remain spiritually astute."[11] Sociologist Christian Smith observed, "The religion and spirituality of most teenagers actually strike us as very powerfully reflecting the contours, priorities, expectations and structures of the larger adult world into which adolescents are being socialized."[12] Gabe Lyons and David Kinnaman, authors of *Unchristian*, found that young adults were interested in spirituality and specifically Jesus, but were having trouble seeing the connection to the modern church.[13] In the nearly ten years since the research and writing of these experts, the teens they studied have become adults. Since their analysis, young adults are observed "cutting the cord" that tethered their culture to that of their parents, including the cultural ties of their faith to traditional expressions of their parents' faith. It seems that they are in some sort of deconstruction phase related to their personal perspectives about spirituality. The deconstruction manifests itself in some young Christians as a search for, to them, a *purer* expression of Christianity. Leading author and lecturer, Phyllis Tickle has described this as a young adult's attempt at finding a spiritual center. She feels that Millennials are peeling away the external layers and fluff of the church to discover the "anchor" that helps them live the lives they are living.[14]

Young adults seem to be searching for moments with God. Interestingly enough, they are searching for these moments detached from the traditional landmarks of faith. And if recent studies by Barna are true, who can blame them, as people who attend church appear no different in behaviors tied to morals and values than people who do not attend church. Their radar is always operating, ever scanning for the possibilities of a special moment with God. Their search begins first, ironically, away from the church. Worship for some young believers is not limited to the exclusivity of the physical or cultural boundaries established by the church. Why are young believers moving away from the traditional expressions of faith? Maybe it is a matter of applicability. They are trying to see how faith applies to their lives. This search for a significant moment is in response to their perceptions of a church that is culturally and spiritually irrelevant, therefore opening the door to deconstruction of traditional orthodoxy.

Bottom line: young adults are leaving the church and may not be coming back. Does that concern you? It does me. Statistics like the ones I mentioned above can make the Builder and Boomer generations feel like complete failures. Thankfully, not all the news is discouraging. When I look around, I see some things that give me hope. The young generation has an affinity toward altruistic ventures—they want to change the world while buying shoes and sunglasses. They want to make a difference in the world, not just "see" the world. A typical young adult has a desire to know spiritual truths. He or she is searching for a connection with God. Young people need a community, thus there is a significant percentage of the younger generation who has stayed involved in the church. In the following chapters we will discuss ways that we can make a difference.

QUESTIONS FOR DISCUSSION

1. Do you see a decline in young adult attendance in your local church? When you think about the young adults closest to you who are not attending church, why have they stopped?
2. How are young adults around you expressing their spirituality? How does this affect the church?

CHAPTER THREE

ALL IS NOT LOST

Tom Crites

"Some major denominations are entering a crisis of existence, losing ground and, in particular, apparently doubting their very own mission." The cultural observer continued, "Both in Europe and in the United States, old-time certainties indeed have vanished and people are increasingly forced to make individual choices as the number of religious and spiritual options are increasing substantially, not the least because of the strong wind of renewal blowing over America."[15] No, this expert was not talking about today—but talking about 1968. I have to admit, I took liberties and changed the past tense to present tense in this quote from Findley Edge, but I did it for a good reason. Why do I bring this to your attention in a book about helping young adults stay connected to church? Because today's new cultural vibes (to use a 1960s word) are very similar to those the church was experiencing in the 1960s. Yes, Baby Boomers were dealing with some of the same issues that their children and grandchildren are facing today. The issues may be in slightly different packages, but they are some of the same issues. I am optimistic that all is not lost and the end results will be as fruitful for these young adults as they have been for the Boomers.

We are in an interesting time in the life of the church. Our situation might best be illustrated as a relay race, even more specifically the moment in a relay race when a baton is passed from one runner to the next. I think we are experiencing the passing of the baton from the Boomer generation to the next largest generation. Unfortunately, the hand-off is anything but a smooth transition. Our older Boomer leaders are holding on tightly to the baton, while our younger leaders are sprinting out of the gate missing the hand-off. As a result, we are losing pace in the race. I believe the core issue at play in the mishandled transfer is the issue of *trust*. Young adults are not 100% sure they want to inherit the current church from the older adults. They are not sure they trust the motives and heart behind the structures and institutions. Older adults are not sure they can trust the younger adults to value the church the way they have–the structures and institutions that they have built with their blood, sweat, and tears. Can I declare a brief respite from the race to offer a statement of understanding? God is sovereign and it is His will that we all are seeking. With that in mind, we have to place our faith in the only One who is trustworthy. We must pray that the Lord will guide our transitions and use us to glorify His name. If you are an older adult, step back and give the upcoming generation what you as a young Baby Boomer wanted–a chance. Young adult, take time to thank those who came before you, honor them for their commitments, and understand that they did their best to follow the Lord.

So let's start here: I am sure that the same God who guided our leaders will continue to direct the next generation's leaders I believe that through God, young people can leverage the influence of the church in ways of reaching the world that we have never imagined. I believe that this young generation has a lot to offer the church. With these things presupposed, let us consider this next generation. Of course there will be anomalies and exceptions, but taking a helicopter tour of this group may be very beneficial. What are people saying about some of the positive dynamics that new leaders are bringing to the table? You will see the characteristics in bold print to make it easier for you to view, study, and consider how your church might take advantage in an effort to be more effective at reaching this group.

This is a very **large group** of people, the largest generation since the Baby Boomers. Sociologists and marketers have estimated the Baby Boomer generation to total approximately 80 million people, while this new generation is topping 70 million. It is estimated that young adults outnumbered Baby Boomers by mid-2015. Due to the size of the cohort they are often referred to as the echo Boomers. The generation between these two, sometimes known as Generation X–The Lost Generation–has nearly half the population of their children.[16] Young adults are going to make major impacts on church culture if not in their numbers alone.

In general, they are **technologically minded**. I remember when my high school received its first personal computer. We had only one, an Apple 2e, and it was set up in the math teacher's room. Students had to sign up for fifteen-minute segments to have the opportunity to tinker with it. Now, only thirty years later, young adults do not know a world without computer driven technology. They assume that the internet was always there. 97% own a computer, 94% own a cell phone, 92% report multitasking while engaging in online communication and exploring the internet.[17] Ask any young adult about their personal devices and they will show you at least two computers or computer-driven devices, which they carry in their backpacks and in their pockets! The internet has become an extension of their personalities so much so that they cannot "unplug." I agree with my pastor friend, Andy Childs of Ebenezer Baptist church in Toccoa, Georgia. He has observed that through constant connections young adults have acquired a hyper-awareness of believers behaving badly. They have front row online seats to the shattering of shame and modesty boundaries by those claiming to be Christians. Because they grew up with the tools, they are not intimidated by technology. They are equipped to use computers and the internet to work smarter and faster than their older colleagues. They will be the first generation to live cradle to grave in a digital age. Let that soak in a bit.

Recent studies show a decrease in religious affiliation of young adults, but that may not tell the whole story. A unique quality of Millennials, in general, is **skepticism toward established institutions**. This directly impacts churches, denominations, and "religion." Barna researchers completed an extensive study focusing on the spirituality of young adults, and found a growing group of religious wanderers.[18] In the Barna study, many Millennials are described as nomads, prodigals, and exiles. They are disillusioned by the current brand of church. I guess no one can really blame them;

they see "Christians" living lives that are no different than the non-Christians in their world. One can imagine the internal dialogue as they ask themselves, "Why should I be a part of an institution that does not make a difference?" While a typical young adult may skip church services, avoid church membership, and deny religious affiliation, it does not mean that they are not spiritually minded. Researchers find that the vast majority of this generation expresses a **strong sense of faith**.[19] Some believe that the percentage that talk to God and lean on religion varies little from the last generation to this.[20] If that is true, and I believe it may very well be, then as this cohort grows older, they will express an even higher percentage of faith than their fathers. This optimistic prediction is based on the fact that, in general, people develop a greater sense of faith as they grow older. One could say that a typical young adult is **searching for answers**, but that search is not limited to the traditional faith paths. Think of the impact we could have if they were to find what they are looking for in church. It may sound funny to consider that they could find it anywhere other than the church, but they are compelled to look for answers everywhere. In my opinion, young adults want the real deal—a focus on what is driven by *life-change* rather than what some may consider "cool" or "effective."

Another dynamic at work in this group is their **sense of entrepreneurship**. Perhaps out of their distrust of the establishment, young adults are seeking to carve out their niche. Instead of relying on the proven organizations and institutions traditionally leading culture, they want to develop their own institutions. Opportunities to make a mark may be more accessible to today's young entrepreneur than they were for former pioneers, as the world has become less "cookie cutter" and more individualized.

New technologies have opened the door to uncharted segments and micro-needs. For example, currently there are 2.5 million different applications (apps) available for cell phone use. Each app is a unique problem solver available to an individual who customizes his or her phone for personal satisfaction. The number of apps has been growing since 2007 when smart phones started becoming more widely available. In the fall of 2008, when interested parties began to track the number of apps, there were only 10,000. But this explosion is really not a surprise; we have been experiencing an obvious push toward individualism in corporate America for at least a decade. I remember when you could have a Coke, Diet Coke, or a Sprite to drink with your cheeseburger. Now, you have the choice of hundreds of soft drinks and flavors from one drink machine in your local fast food restaurant.

These examples are related to the spirit of entrepreneurship in young adults. They have been brought up in a world where they did not have to "settle." They have always been able to have exactly what they wanted. **They have been encouraged to branch out, experiment, and get creative**. This has impacted the church in many ways already. The number of parachurch organizations has exploded, each organization designed to meet a specific need, possibly in a specific area of the world. More often than not, these organizations offer an individual a laser focus ministry opportunity. If a person feels led to serve the orphans in Iceland, there are a number of organizations that are thus focused and ready to assist. The internet has allowed for these organizations to communicate needs to a wider audience, allowing for broader representation and support. I imagine that the spirit of entrepreneurship coupled with an aversion for established institutions, supported by ever-expanding technology and global access, will continue to yield new and different solutions to the evils of the world.

In addition to this spirit of entrepreneurship there is a **bent toward altruism**. This is seen in the number of social-impact initiatives that have popped up in the last several years. Young adults are not interested in just seeing the world; they want to change the world. And, why should they believe that they cannot change the world? They have been told their whole lives that they are special and can do anything. Companies are finding a market ready for the buyer who wants to change the world. Tom's, a fledgling shoe company, became a powerhouse through the "buy a pair, give a pair" campaign. Tom's has continued their social entrepreneurship through the sale of sunglasses, clothing, blankets, and more. It is just one of dozens of corporations expressing a value aimed at social impact. Young adults are finding flecks of satisfaction through their coffee purchases, eye exams, software downloads, and so on. Why are they so open to these types of ventures? I think all of this is related to the age-old question: "What is the meaning of life?" Young adults have lived through the

Great Recession; they have seen their parents and grandparents suffer from the stresses of financial losses and foreclosures. Seeing that money cannot produce happiness, they have turned to a *sense of meaning* as the catalyst for fulfillment. Young adults have expressed that feeling purposeful is more important than feeling happy.[21] This is manifesting as a deeper sense of selflessness.

Another dynamic molding the younger generation is the fact that they are **seeking deep relationships**. Considering the status to their culture, young adults may have lost the meaning of "relationship." They have hundreds, even thousands, of virtual "friends" to whom they feed information on a regular basis through social media. They have people following their lives as they post pictures and witty banter via virtual communities. They are constantly connected to their electronic world through their cell phones and computers. John Palfrey and Urs Gasser, authors of *Born Digital* write,

> "Those who were born digital do not remember a world in which letters were printed and sent, much less handwritten, or where people met up at formal dances rather than on Facebook. The changing nature of human relationships is second nature to some, and learned behavior to others. But in the course of this relentless connectivity, the very nature of relationships—even what it means to 'befriend' someone—is changing. Online friendships are based on many of the same things as traditional friendships—shared interests, frequent interaction— but they nonetheless have a very different tenor: they are often fleeting; they are easy to enter into and easy to leave, without so much as a goodbye; and they are also perhaps enduring in ways we have yet to understand."[22]

I believe one result that we are seeing today is a **strong desire for** what a young adult might refer to as "**authentic community**." This is probably bubbling up from the fact that one can be inauthentic and get away with it online. An example is the phenomenon called "catfishing." This is when a person is tricked, usually through online media, into a relationship with a person who does not exist in reality. The online "person" is a creation of a real user who chooses not to reveal his or her true identity. Young adults have found the internet a convenient place to connect with people, but they have developed a guard that protects them from common scammers. Thus, you hear a millennial discuss his or her need for an authentic community. Some describe this community as a place where they can be their "real" selves. In this authentic community they can find safety, be vulnerable, and receive support facing the challenges of life. A popular spiritual guide, Henri Nouwen, once wrote,

> "Community is first of all a quality of the heart. It grows from the spiritual knowledge that we are alive not for ourselves but for one another. Community is the fruit of our capacity to make the interests of others more important than our own... The question, therefore, is not 'How can we make community?' but 'How can we develop and nurture giving hearts?'"[23]

I believe that young adults feel a pull toward community in a response to the self-centeredness of social media. It is as if Millennials seek community to balance themselves. If you are a parent or a pastor, I hope you can see the tremendous opportunities in facilitating "authentic community."

Ladies and gentlemen, the helicopter tour is over. As you read this chapter, you hopefully identified more traits and attitudes that are contributors to this new generation's mindset. It is safe to say that their identity is still developing. There are other dynamics that will come into focus as they begin to take their places in leadership. I believe these are the main ones that are influencing church culture today. If we could peer into the future maybe ten years from now, imagine the impact this cohort could have for the gospel, if they stay. For those in leadership feeling tentative about handing off the baton, I want to encourage you to consider the possibilities. The next generation is going to be a powerful one. Let us do all we can now to encourage them to stay and not stray from the church.

QUESTIONS FOR DISCUSSION

1. Which of these dynamics impact your church most now and why?

2. Do you know of another trait or attitude that is becoming pervasive in the next generation of adults? Does that worry or excite you about the future? Why?

3. How might a young adult help your ministry? Where can you see a young adult making positive enhancements in your church?

4. What are some steps that a pastor or parent can take to help facilitate a smoother transition?

5. How has your church changed in an effort to reach the next generation?

CHAPTER FOUR

SURVEY SAYS

Tom Crites

We must not hide them from their children,
but must tell a future generation
the praises of the Lord,
His might, and the wonderful works He has performed.
(Psalms 78:4 HCSB)

What a blessing and a tremendous responsibility to say the least. I am amazed that God would entrust the propagation of His story into the shaky hands of the human race. Honestly, humans have not done much correctly over the years and it seems that we are failing miserably at transmitting God's truths to the next generations. I, for one, am not happy with the status quo. I believe that we can and must do a better job of passing along our faith. Well known Bible commentator, Matthew Henry stated our task well, "Our great care must be to lodge our religion, that great deposit, pure and entire, in the hands of those that succeed us."[24] Hopefully, if you are reading this book, you would agree that every Christian bears the responsibility of faith transmission. It just makes sense—if we do not do the job, no one will. It is with that responsibility in mind and the urgency of the times, that this research project was set in motion.

There have been many studies focused on the people who are currently outside the church, including people who have left the church, the church dropouts, the non-attenders, and the unbelievers. What about the young adults who have stayed in the church? Across this country, there are literally hundreds of thousands of young adults who have decided to stay in church. This study was designed to focus on them. Their perspectives may help to answer some of the questions church members have when it comes to reaching and keeping young adults.

Our study evaluated the perceptions, attitudes, feelings, and experiences of those who stayed in church to see if there were any identifiable factors that parents and church leaders could use to help keep others from dropping out. The study included information from nearly 1,400 young adults around the country. The participants came from several different denominational backgrounds and traditions. They lived and worked in every type of community from small rural towns to large metropolitan cities. This unique study relied solely upon social media for distribution and promotion, allowing for the desired wired community.

The results confirmed much of what was expected, but there were several surprises and unexpected conclusions. The hope is that through the use of this information, we can see parents, church leaders, and church members reach and keep the younger adults in their community.

Participation in the survey was incredible as 1,391 individuals joined in the study. The number of respondents to the study was ideal for the purpose of the study.

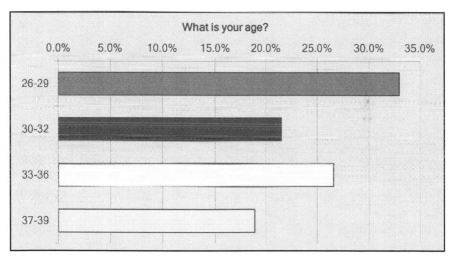

Percentage of Participants by Age

One-third of the participants were in the twenty-six to twenty-nine age range. The other three groups identified were well represented by the remaining two-thirds of those taking the survey. Nearly 80% of those surveyed were under the age of thirty-seven. Over 99% of the participants identified themselves as Christians, and the vast majority, 93%, admitted to being a church member. The young adults taking the survey were from every corner of the United States. Most were from the South and the Midwest, but a significant number of them were from Western and Northeastern regions of the U.S.

Twitter and Facebook were the principal tools used with a web link directing likely parties to the questionnaire. Email contact was used in addition to social media and proved to be a useful tool. Using electronic media to deploy the survey proved to be very beneficial. It kept costs low and allowed for speedy response rates. In addition, leaders representing the top ten denominations in number were contacted and several were gracious in pushing out the survey to those under their leadership influence.

The purpose of this study was to understand if there were significant relationships in the backgrounds and habits of young adults that may have impacted their commitments to stay in church. The survey contained fifty-three questions that ranged from open-ended, multiple choice, ranking and yes/no question types. Needless to say, a mountain of data was produced. For a guy who enjoys digging into data, this was a dream come true. Still, there was the challenge of how one might get his arms around what all this information meant. I selected a statistical method called a factor analysis to help guide the in-depth study. This process distilled the information, identifying the main factors at work. The statistical analysis revealed eight areas that required deeper investigation. I followed this process with a series of comparisons, focused on the variables within the main factors, to study significant differences. Upon further review, the data told the story of fifteen significant issues. I believe that these issues are incredibly important to the future of our churches.

I pray that as you read about each of these issues, you will decide to do all you can to "tell the next generation." These identified elements address foundational, contextual essentials that can prepare the way for the transfer of the faith. Think of them this way: when I decided that I wanted to propose to my wife, I visualized the perfect setting.

I mentally picked out my suit and tie, imagined the romantic dinner, and rehearsed what I would say in my proposal. I purchased the ring and secured the time and place where the big event would occur. I wanted to do all I could to ensure that she would accept my plea to marry. The afternoon before the "big day," I secured her engagement ring. It was a beautiful expression of my love for her and exactly what she wanted. As soon as I picked up the ring, I became overwhelmed with excitement and could not wait to ask her to be my wife. So instead of the romantic evening, my proposal came while we were sharing in the housework at her mother's home. Thankfully she said yes in spite of my blunder. We still went on our romantic date and enjoyed a time of dreaming about the future. I realized that the real preparations had been made during the three years that we dated. I did not need to manufacture a context in which she would yield to my will; it had already been prepared. Based on our three years together, she knew that my love and desire to spend my life with her were real.

As you read each of the following chapters, consider them as preparation for your proposal to your children and your children's children. This information can help you express your love and your desire for them to stay in church and grow in their faith. This information can set the context for the wonderful proposal every child is destined to experience. And when the time comes for them to decide to stay or stray, I pray they will decide to stay.

QUESTIONS FOR DISCUSSION

1. Why is it important for parents to impart the faith to the next generation?
2. Some people say that they "want to let their kids make their own decisions" regarding church. What are the dangers of this position?
3. How can a pastor encourage a person who feels like they have not done a good job transferring the faith to the next generation?
4. What can you do to study young adults in your community and congregation in order to discover ways to be more effective in meeting their needs?

CHAPTER FIVE

GUIDING PRINCIPLES

Steve Parr

T he word "context" means the circumstances that form the setting for an event, statement, or idea, and in terms of which it can be fully understood and assessed. To understand the research we are presenting and to benefit fully, you need to understand four principles that give context to the study and the findings. Though brief, the next few pages are critical as a backdrop, and the possibility for misinterpretation is much higher if the data is interpreted outside of the context of the following.

God's Grace

Repentance. Saving faith. Atonement. Justification. Grace. Adoption. Salvation. Regeneration. Sanctification. Perseverance. All of these terms are significant when you delve into issues of soteriology or the study of salvation. What distinguishes one who has a genuine personal relationship with the Lord Jesus Christ and one who does not? What are the consequences for those who possess a genuine "saving faith" compared to one who has rejected the gospel or a person who made the decision to join a local church but never repented of sin?

The simplest explanation for why young adults are still active in church could be argued that they are genuine followers of Jesus. They have truly repented of their sins, having placed their faith in Jesus Christ for forgiveness and salvation. They have been made righteous by the atoning death of Jesus upon the cross and the reality of His resurrection. Their lives have been changed by the power of the Holy Spirit and they possess a faith that has led them to an intimate, growing relationship with Jesus Christ.

God's grace is not a principle, but is the unmerited favor of God. Books have been written on all of these issues related to soteriology, and resources are plentiful for dissecting the nuances of all of these terms and their implications. The principle of God's grace in the context of this study is an acknowledgement that salvation is a work of God. We cannot "save" anyone from their sins. Only God can do that.

While believing wholeheartedly in God's saving grace and His power to sustain the faith of those who truly become followers of Jesus Christ, you cannot ignore the dynamics of the influences that appear to drive children and teens toward a faith that includes service and involvement in the local church into their adult life. None of the study or conclusions that you will read is intended in any way to minimize or contradict the ultimate factor in faith which is God's saving grace. You will be encouraged by what you will discover to do all in your power to provide an environment which is most conducive for children and teens to develop openness to God with a prayerful spirit, acknowledging that it is indeed God that is the critical factor in one's faith.

Probabilities

Suppose you were getting ready to book a flight for a trip across the ocean. Prior to making your purchase you come across a news story that contains some eye-opening research. Two airlines fly out of your local airport: Alpha Airlines and Omega Airlines. You much prefer Alpha Airlines but discover that the probability based on past history is that you have only a 96% chance of making it to your destination safely. Omega Airlines, on the other hand, has a record that suggests that they can get you there safely over 99.6% of the time. Which airline would you be more inclined to choose?

I don't know about you, but I would set aside my initial preference for Alpha and go with Omega because this could be a life-or-death decision. Keep in mind that both airlines can get you safely to the destination. Also note that there is no guarantee that you will arrive safely no matter which airline you choose. I would select the airline that has a definitive greater probability of arriving safely over the other airline.

What if I discovered that children who grow up in church and wear blue on Fridays when they are young are twice as likely to actively serve in the local church when they reach thirty years of age than the person who wears colors other than blue on Fridays? Although that piece of data would not make a lot of sense to me, I would be inclined to lay out blue for my children on Thursday nights because I want to do all that I can to provide whatever is needed for them to become a lifelong disciple of Jesus Christ.

The guiding principle of probability is an acknowledgement that some issues over which you and I have influence tend to provide the best environment for a healthy and sustainable faith. We need to understand what those issues are and make changes where necessary to provide the proper environment because the spiritual health of our children is at stake. The good news is that you will discover that most, if not all, of the issues discerned from the research do make sense. But, even if they don't, change what you must to help the faith of the younger generation in your family and your church to flourish and to last into their adult lives.

Exceptions

"Yes, but...." Have you ever made a statement like that? Yes, Alpha Airlines has experienced several crashes, but I have flown on it a dozen times and have never experienced a problem. Yes, Omega Airlines has an almost flawless record, but my uncle died in a crash the very first time that he flew with them.

The principle of exceptions is to remind you that anyone can find anecdotal examples of people who grew up with exactly the opposite environment of what will be described and it worked out just fine. Anyone can quickly point out a person who grew up with great Christian parents, attended a vibrant church, and proceeded to drop out of school, become a drug addict, commit a horrendous crime, and is now in prison with a life sentence. That is a good example of the principle of exceptions. These exceptions happen, however he or she may of had nine peers who grew up with great families and attended the same church. Though none of them turned out perfectly, none ended up with a life sentence in prison. That situation was an exception.

Be aware of this principle as you discover the factors that make a difference in whether those who grew up in church are still attending as adults. Be careful not to focus on the exceptions as you examine the research. Focus instead on changes, adjustments, or affirmations of your actions that best provide an environment for a faith that sustains into one's life as an adult.

Responsibilities

The research that you will be introduced to is all about the principle of responsibilities. Every person is subject to the influence of other people and the circumstances they encounter throughout their lives. Everyone has influence over others, making their own decisions critical since those in their sphere may choose the same path. Though horrid, the issue of abuse is a great way to illustrate this principle. Childhood and adolescence represent the phases of life where humans develop attitudes, morals, perspectives, and direction for their lives. The child who is abused is at such a great disadvantage over the child who grows up in a healthy home. The good news is that many who are abused overcome the wrongs that were experienced as children. In contrast, some who grow up in great homes with loving parents go on to make terrible decisions that ruin their lives as adults.

What is my responsibility? I need to provide an environment for my children free of abuse. Not only is that the right thing to do, but the decision to do so gives my girls the best opportunity to live healthy and productive lives as adults. There are no guarantees, but I do have a responsibility.

As you discover the principles that tend to make the greatest difference in the spiritual development of those who are growing up, you have a responsibility. The responsibility does not belong to parents alone. Many of the issues relate to life in the church. Sadly, many churches have unhealthy environments because of wrong attitudes, unwillingness to change, poor leadership, or traditions that actually hinder the discipleship of the younger generation. As you proceed and discover the factors that make a difference, please do so with the commitment to take responsibility.

One more thing needs to be done before you study the factors that make the greatest difference for those who stay in church. The results also revealed a few surprises regarding issues that we thought mattered, but actually had little, if any, influence at all over whether a young adult who grew up in church still actively attends. Let's now consider what those issues were.

CHAPTER SIX

FIRST SURPRISE

Steve Parr

The point of the study of young adults who grew up in church and stayed was to determine what dynamics could commonly be identified that tend to lead to a lifetime commitment to Jesus and active involvement in the life of a local church. You will soon discover fifteen major factors that were discovered which make a huge difference, and some were surprising. Another surprise was that some issues did not make as big of a difference as I would have thought. Let's take a few moments to discuss five issues that didn't seem to affect whether or not a young adult who grew up in church had strayed or stayed active as an adult.

Parents from Differing Denominational Backgrounds

What happens in a circumstance where mom grew up as a Methodist and dad grew up as a Presbyterian? What about if dad was Pentecostal and mom was Baptist? Or what if mom was Lutheran and dad was Wesleyan? Don't take offense if your denomination was left out, because the potential combinations could fill up a book much less a chapter. The common factor is that each of these denominations, as well as others that could be included, is centered on a faith relationship with Jesus Christ and the belief that the Bible is the Word of God.

However, styles of worship, emphases and various interpretations of certain doctrines, the organizational structure of the churches, and in some cases nomenclature varies, not only from denomination to denomination but also between local churches belonging to the same denomination. Is that not a potentially confusing scenario to children that could become a hindrance to the development of their faith?

Notice that the parents described in these circumstances are not from different religious backgrounds, but a parent would still be wise to consider whether opposing convictions based on denominational experiences might be detrimental to the development of the faith of their children. I encountered a gentleman recently and asked him about his "church home." He replied, "What are you talking about?" "Where do you and your family attend church?" I asked.

He went on to explain that he and his wife were from different religious backgrounds. I was curious how they were rearing their children regarding matters of faith. The result was that since they were from different religious backgrounds they had elected to go to neither church. They were totally disconnected to any congregation. What are the probabilities that their sons and daughters will be attending church when they are adults? It will take a miracle for their children to ever get connected.

The research revealed that there was no correlation between the parents' denominational background (that is, being from the same denomination) and their children's active participation in church once they became adults. But here is the key point: the survey was of young adults who grew up attending church, meaning that the parents had come to a consensus. Either one of the parents deferred or they both changed and settled in with a new local church. When parents from different denominational backgrounds determine that the best solution is not to go at all, then they are likely ensuring that their children will not grow as followers of Christ. Being from different denominational backgrounds is not detrimental, but failure to express faith through attendance and service in a local church is injurious to the faith of the children.

Having a Youth Pastor While Growing Up

Another surprise to me was that there was no connection between having a youth pastor on staff during one's teen years and whether or not that person was active in church as an adult. Being a former youth pastor myself, it might be easy to take offense at this point. No need for that. The study revealed several positive relationships between a healthy youth ministry experience and the likelihood that someone who grew up in church stayed when they became adults.

The research did reveal that if one had a youth pastor, the relationship with him or her was significant. You will discover later that those who had youth leaders they liked tended to stay as adults, and if they did not like them they tended to have strayed. A deeper look at this point will reveal that it is actually positive rather than negative. It is not a poor reflection on the role of a youth pastor as much as a correlation to the size of churches.

Take my denomination, the Southern Baptist Convention, as an example in Georgia where I live. Only 25% of the churches have a youth pastor on staff. If the role of a youth pastor were essential in connecting someone into their adult years, then the children and students from 75% of our churches would be doomed to a failing faith. The good news is your church does not have to have a youth pastor in order for the faith of your children to thrive. On the other hand, if you do have one and your children have a positive relationship with him or her, it can enhance their faith.

Congregations that have the resources to employ staff members who can give attention to the faith development of students are blessed and should take advantage of the opportunity. In the absence of those resources, volunteers who are willing to invest spiritually into the lives of middle school and high school students can equally make a great impact. Although having a youth pastor did not correlate with whether one stayed connected as an adult, having sufficient activities for students while growing up did prove to make a difference in one staying or straying. Having a staff youth pastor is good, but having a ministry focused on students is essential. Find a way to minister to students no matter what size church you attend.

The Type of School Attended in Elementary, Middle, and High School

Most parents are very passionate about the type of education their children receive when growing up, and rightly so. Should you send your children to a public school and expose them to a diverse expression of morality, beliefs, and religious expressions? Is it better to allow them to be light in the darkness or to protect them from the negative influences they will be exposed to? Perhaps you should send them to a private school where academic expectations are higher and standards are more strictly enforced. Would you do better to place your child in an atmosphere that minimizes some of the negative influence, although admittedly does not eliminate it?

Perhaps as a parent you should more specifically place your child in a private Christian school to maximize their exposure to consistent doctrinal instruction as well as a good academic environment where you know that the teachers reflect your values. You may have a conviction that home schooling is the best course to take to buffer your children against much of the negative influence and to remove many of the distractions to their academic development. I am generalizing at this point and have no intent to misinterpret why you may or may not have a feeling about any one of these approaches or objections to the other.

However, the research brought a bit of a surprise at this point. No correlation was revealed between which of these school environments one grew up in and whether they were active in church as adults. If you have a strong belief about any one of these approaches to education, you are to be commended and should carry on with that conviction. But it is not the key to the development of your child's faith. I am not saying it is unimportant but that it is not the "key." You will soon discover fifteen other issues that were critical, and it is interesting to see that on the college level there is more of a correlation. What happens in the home and in the local church appear to trump the educational environment (public, private, private Christian, or home school) in regard to influence over whether one strays or stays in church as an adult. Follow your convictions on this, but do not rely on the school your child attends to give them the roots they need to stay faithful into their adult lives.

Participation in a New Christians Class

Various denominations use different terms for this experience, but in essence it reflects several hours of equipping and education to help a new young believer understand the essentials of faith and doctrine. Participation is a rite of passage in some faith traditions provided at a particular age, while in others it is available at whatever point a child, or in some circumstances teens or adults, express their desire to become a follower of Jesus Christ. An introductory discipleship experience such as this is commendable and important, and any church would do well to offer an orientation experience for young believers. However, no correlation was noted between whether one did or did not attend such a class and whether or not they stayed in church as adults.

The point of this finding is not that a church should not offer such an experience. I believe that they absolutely should offer this class, and if your church does not, you need to find a way to make it happen. However, you cannot confine one's discipleship experience to a four, six, or eight hour class. A *New Christians* class or the equivalent by any other name is an introduction to discipleship, and Christian education and spiritual maturity cannot be conferred by a certificate. Discipleship is a lifelong journey. Offer the *New Christians* class, but also be sure to determine what comes next. Simply providing a *New Christians* class does not result in a lifetime commitment to serve Christ in a local church.

Faith of the Grandparents

My grandparents had a very positive and direct influence over my faith development. Perhaps you would say the same thing. However, the research revealed that the faith of grandparents, though positive, had a minimal correlation over whether one had strayed or stayed in church as an adult. Like some points made earlier, this is not a negative reflection on grandparents but a reality that parents must understand.

As a parent you cannot delegate the spiritual development of your children to your parents. Though they may love grandpa and grandma dearly, they look to you as a parent for the ultimate validation for whether faith is real and relevant. Although your parents, your children's grandparents, may have said "yes" to faith in God, their opinion is invalidated when mom or dad lives a life that communicates "no" to the reality or relevance of faith in Christ.

What should a grandparent do? I advise that you do anything and everything you can to strengthen and develop the faith of your grandchildren. The greater point is for the parent. You are the primary influence and your child is inclined to follow you into eternity. Where will you be? I want my children to go to heaven one day and although I appreciate anything my parents or my wife's parents might add, I am taking responsibility for modeling, teaching, and encouraging my children to have an authentic and growing personal relationship with Jesus Christ. How about you?

QUESTIONS FOR DISCUSSION

1. Which of these was the greatest surprise to you and why?
2. Do you know of another issue that people tend to overemphasize that may not make as big of a difference as one may think in whether a child who grows up in church stays?
3. What actions should your church take to strengthen ministry to students, whether you have a youth pastor or not?
4. What is the process in your church for orienting new believers and how can it be improved?

PART TWO

FIFTEEN ISSUES THAT MATTERED GREATLY

CHAPTER SEVEN

I HAVE DECIDED TO FOLLOW JESUS

Tom Crites

I love Sundays in autumn! It probably has to do with my childhood memories of jumping into piles of leaves, sandlot football games with the kids in the neighborhood, and cool nights that called for a jacket. I recall one particular Sunday in October when I was eight. My family and I had just arrived home from the Woodmar Restaurant where I had enjoyed my usual cream of chicken and rice soup, roll, and side of jello. We were settling into our Sunday afternoon routines of naps and TV, but an unsettling mood kept me from enjoying the Masterpiece Theatre's broadcast of *Abbott and Costello*. It was because that morning in church, we had heard from an evangelist. I had listened intently, maybe for the first time ever in a service, as he read from the Scripture and told his engaging stories. My mind felt compelled to respond to his invitation at the end of the meeting, but I could not convince my feet to step out from the pew.

Now at home, I again felt compelled to do something. Meekly, I left the den of our home and entered my parents' room where they seemed already engaged in their nap. I touched my mother's arm and waited for her eyes to open. "What's wrong?" she whispered. "I need to be saved," was my response. Holding my parents' hands, I knelt beside the bed and asked Jesus into my heart. I announced my decision to follow Jesus that evening after another stirring message by our guest evangelist. The next Sunday, I was baptized as my immediate family and friends looked on. It is hard to believe that forty years have passed since that October Sunday; it seems like such a short time ago. The transformation that I experienced that afternoon has left a permanent impression on my memory. I had stepped out of sin's grasp and into the arms of my merciful Lord.

I wish I could say that my spiritual journey has been focused and productive since that unforgettable day of my eighth year, but honestly it has not. I have experienced my share of ups and downs. I have stood on spiritual mountaintops and have felt trapped in the muck of my valleys. I imagine many have the same story. When I reflect on my spiritual highs and lows, I always return to that October Sunday. You see, I had a life-changing experience that day. It was so real and profound that I have remained sure in my salvation since then. That experience has served as a tether, keeping me from floating off into a spiritual black hole.

Young adults who have stayed in church indicated that they have had similar experiences. Not surprisingly, over two-thirds said that they were younger than thirteen when they came into a relationship with Jesus. Over three-fourths testified that they were younger than sixteen when they committed their lives to Jesus. Those high percentages reveal several things about today's young adults who grew up attending church. First, most of them were exposed to the gospel at a young age. I would assume that their parents involved them in a variety of children's and youth activities and programs where they would be told the story of Jesus and the cross. They were probably given the opportunity to reflect upon the gospel in addition to the chance to respond. They, like me, have a memory catalogued in their brain as the "salvation experience" that they point to as the moment that they came into a spiritual relationship with Christ.

For a parent, this should sound a loud alarm because 75% of the adults in the survey said they accepted Christ before age sixteen. You do not have much time! Research has shown that people are more likely to accept Christ as a child than they are as an adult. Some have reported that the probability of a person experiencing salvation in adulthood is only 6%.[25] It is imperative that parents expose their children to the gospel. They should find a Bible-teaching local church and regularly take their children to learn the stories of the faith. They should read the Bible and Bible stories to their children, allowing them to grow in their comprehension of spiritual truths. Parents should allow their child to hear the gospel presented and preached. I personally believe that a parent should share the gospel with their child. I had the privilege of leading my children to the Lord. I am very glad that I had the opportunity to share in that experience with them as my parents shared in that experience with me.

Pastors should be hearing the alarm just as loudly. As a child grows up attending the local church, the pastor may have the attention of that child for an hour a week for ten years. That is equal to only about 500 hours (at most). That is not enough time to create an environment focused upon the spiritual development of a child. Pastors must strategically plan for occasions where children are presented the gospel. They need to think creatively about children's Bible study times and special events. I am a proponent of Vacation Bible School (VBS). When conducted correctly, it can be a tremendous tool for reaching children with the gospel. If you are not currently scheduling a VBS, taking kids to a VBS, or participating in a VBS in your community, plan on doing it next summer. Children love these programs. In our culture, VBS may be the best tool for reaching children with the gospel.

Pastors, please hear what I am saying: get strategic about sharing the gospel with children in your mission field. You do not have to offer a VBS. Have a kid's camp, a children's musical, fun night, or holiday party–plan whatever you feel fits best at your church. If you will put it on the calendar, it is more likely to happen. I want to encourage you to plan a week every summer for VBS or some equivalent alternative. Find a man or woman in the church who has a heart for reaching children. Ask them to take leadership of the VBS or alternate activity that you propose. Work to get as many people as possible to volunteer for the week. Go all out in promotion with the aim to get every child in the neighborhood there. Lead your congregation to pray for the souls of the people involved. Boldly share the gospel with every child in attendance. Why? Because this is what is evident from the research: we have a brief window of opportunity to share the gospel with our children. Adults who accepted Christ as children are more likely to stay in church.

Another interesting facet of this issue focuses on the lower end of the age "window." An interesting difference was observed in those who strayed versus those who stayed. If a young adult identified that they were younger than six when they came into a relationship with Jesus, they were 32% more likely to stray from church later in life. Let us take a moment to consider what may be happening in the lives of those who identified a preschool faith experience. Before we travel too far down this road, I want you to understand that I believe people can become Christians very early in life. I have heard testimonies of Christian leaders that point to a conversion experience as early as three.[26] I am not saying that it cannot happen. Salvation can and does come to very young children. Most children are a bit older when they experience salvation. For those who testify to a preschool conversion and are straying from the church, a few things may be happening. They may not actually be Christians. Only God knows this, but possibly they have never truly experienced salvation, and now, as a young adult outside the influence of parents and friends, there is no conviction to be in church. One should surely examine his own heart to determine if he is actually convinced that he is an authentic believer.

Another issue here is that young children may not remember the "spiritual moment." Maybe the experience came too early for their memory. Fourteen percent of the young adults who strayed from the church said that they were baptized as an infant. In these cases, the individual could not have remembered the event and so it is not helping to tether them to their faith. Other participants pointed to a contextual misunderstanding of the purpose for baptism. Five percent of those who strayed said that they were baptized before their salvation experience. You will discover some interesting insights on this issue in the next chapter.

Young adults who stay in church have had an experience that they point to as the moment of their salvation. When asked the open-ended question, "Why have you stayed in church?" twenty percent of the responses by those who stayed pointed to a personal salvation experience. Most of them had a memorable experience as a child who was supported by "family upbringing" (first most common reply to an open-ended question) and "development while young" (the eighth most common reply). They have found that experience to be an important marker in their spiritual journey.

A Word for Parents

You cannot make your child accept Christ. But as a parent, you can encourage a child in the development of their faith by offering them opportunities to hear the gospel and learn the stories of the faith. I believe the best place to do that is the home. The second most important place to offer these opportunities is a Bible-teaching church. Believe me, I have experienced the fatigue of parenting. I have collapsed into bed exhausted from trying to provide and care for my family. I know that parenting is hard work. I also know how quickly it passes. Parents, take time to share your faith with your children: read Bible stories to them, take them to church events, and pray with them. Do everything in your power to create an environment that will pave the way for their salvation. Then, when they experience that "spiritual moment" of transformation, you will be immeasurably happy that you did all you could do.

A Word for Pastors

Take time to plan opportunities for children under your care to hear the gospel. I knew a pastor who would disappear every year the church held VBS. I always thought that he was missing a great chance to see many receive Christ. I know that implementing a week-long ministry like VBS is very challenging and time-intensive. It is expensive, exhausts your volunteers, is hard on your facilities, makes already long days feel longer, and so on. I also know that it is so worth it! I have seen at least one child come to faith during every VBS that I have been a part of. Catch what I am saying here: you do not have to schedule a VBS, but do plan something that creates an opportunity for you to share the gospel with children.

QUESTIONS FOR DISCUSSION

1. Share about your "spiritual moment" when you became a Christian. Why is it important to have this memory?
2. What are some things your parents did that helped you in your faith journey?
3. How can a pastor improve the environment at his church, making the most of opportunities to share the gospel with children?
4. How do we balance sharing the gospel with children without being manipulative or coercive? List some guidelines that you would recommend for sharing the gospel with children.

CHAPTER EIGHT

LET'S GO DOWN TO THE RIVER

Steve Parr

"I baptize you my brother in the name of the Father, of the Son, and of the Holy Spirit, buried with Christ in baptism, raised to walk in newness of life." Those were the words spoken as the pastor gently placed me under the water and stood me back up on the day of my baptism. I made a public profession of my faith and declared to all present my commitment to be a follower of Jesus Christ. Friends and family embraced me later in the service as I stood in front of the congregation along with others who made the same declaration. I remember what I was wearing, the pastor who baptized me, friends and family in attendance, and the emotions I experienced on that day of personal dedication.

Do you remember your baptism? If so, you are much more likely to be fully involved in the life of a local congregation than a person who was never baptized, or a person who was baptized but has no recollection of the experience. In the previous chapter, the importance of spiritual memory was discussed with a focus on the "spiritual moment" when one accepts Christ. The research also revealed that the baptism experience is a significant point and actually correlates to the likelihood that a young adult has stayed in church rather than strayed.

One issue that nearly all Christian denominations hold in common is the significance of the baptism experience and would agree that the Scripture teaches baptism for believers. The diversity of opinion revolves around the mode of baptism, sprinkling or immersion, and the timing of baptism. The issue of timing emerged as one of the greater gaps between young adults who grew up in church and had remained active or dropped out.

My baptism was not the beginning of my faith and discipleship experience. The genesis of my faith was very personal and private. Although I was viewed as a person of good moral character, the Holy Spirit clearly convicted me that I was a sinner. I further understood that my sin separated me from God. The good news is that God sent His only Son, Jesus Christ, into the world, and His death on the cross was not incidental but was intentional. He died on the cross as a sacrifice for my sins. His death was the payment for my sin, and I once read that His resurrection was the receipt. When God brought Him forth from the grave on the third day, He validated that Jesus was indeed His Son and that His sacrifice was sufficient as payment for my sin.

Based on my understanding of who Jesus is and what He did on the cross, I personally repented of my sin and asked Him for forgiveness. Though I was not present when Jesus lived, by faith I believed in His life, death, and resurrection. These things took place in my heart in a very personal way. In much the same way that my wife and I exchanged wedding vows on the day that we were married, I prayed within my heart committing my life to Jesus as the Lord and Savior of my life. The decision was simple, but it was not easy. I wrestled with this within my heart for some time before making the commitment. The circumstances were personal because no one else could do this for me. It was private because it took place within my heart, and though I was in a public setting, no one had any idea what was going on between me and God within my own thoughts. However, I could not keep this experience private.

I began to share my commitment with family members, and on the very next Sunday I responded to a public invitation in my home church at the conclusion of the pastor's sermon. The congregation was delighted and very affirming. I was committed to be a follower of Jesus. What is next? The Bible teaches in the New Testament that followers of Jesus are to believe and then to be baptized. I made arrangements with my pastor to be publicly baptized in obedience to

God's Word. God was working in my life even before I trusted Him as Savior and Lord. The Holy Spirit began to shape my thinking and my actions. Though not perfect by any means, God's guidance in my life was clear and remains so to this day. I feel a deep sense of conviction when I sin and I take great joy in following Christ and serving others through the church which Jesus refers to as His body.

My salvation was the beginning of my journey as a follower of Jesus Christ. My baptism was the first step that I took in obedience to His Word. Both were memorable and critical to my development and to the depth of my commitment. Ninety-three percent of the young adults we surveyed who grew up in church and were still involved as adults stated that either they were "Christians with a commitment to grow in their faith," or "though not perfect, were Christians with a vibrant faith." Less than 7% of those who said they were Christians, "but honestly lacked commitment," were still active as young adults. Only 0.18% were active if they did not claim to have a personal relationship with Jesus.

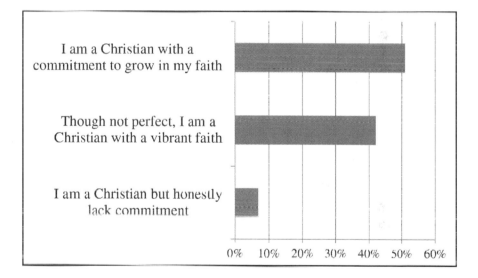

A survey was not necessary to come to that conclusion. Though you may not have the data at hand you would have likely assumed what the information revealed. However, what the study revealed regarding baptism may lead some parents to re-evaluate how they approach this issue with their children depending on their current convictions. The survey asked the young adults who grew up in church about the timing of their baptism. The question asked was: "Which best reflects when you were baptized?" The possible answers were as follows:

> I have not been baptized.
> I was baptized as an infant.
> I was baptized prior to my salvation experience.
> I was baptized soon following my salvation experience.
> I was baptized long after my salvation experience.

The most obvious variable related to those who had never been baptized at all. Those who were never baptized were almost 400% more likely to have strayed as those who were baptized among those who grew up attending church. Should we not simply baptize all of our children if this is the case to increase the likelihood that they will remain faithful? It does not work that way. As a matter of fact, those who are baptized as infants are much more likely to stray than those baptized following their salvation experience. The research revealed that participants baptized as infants were 184% more likely to have strayed from church compared to those who were baptized at an alternate time in their life. The reverse was true of those baptized following a personal salvation experience. While being baptized following one's personal commitment to Christ did not ensure that they were still active, the data revealed that they were much more likely to remain faithful compared to those baptized as infants. Those baptized after salvation were 16.6% more likely to remain active than to have dropped out.

Would it not be great if we could give our children a certificate when they were young with the knowledge that receipt of the document would ensure they were devoted followers of Christ from that point forward for the rest of their lives? But, it does not work that way. God must work in their hearts and as parents we must pray to that end. We model and instruct what it means to have a genuine relationship with God through Jesus Christ. I want to be respectful in my comments to parents and leaders with other traditions regarding baptism. We must be intellectually honest and acknowledge that as parents, pastors, and priests we do not have the authority to confer salvation on anyone. We can encourage and guide, but only God can save someone from their sin.

For those who were baptized as infants or as small children with no personal recollection of the experience, and for those who may have provided such a ceremonial experience for your children, I want to commend you for your desire to seek God's blessing and for your aspiration that your family would follow Christ here on earth and ultimately spend eternity in heaven. The result here is a reminder that men are not made right through ceremonies, but through personal repentance and faith in Jesus Christ resulting in a commitment to His Lordship. You can guide and teach your own kids as well as the children in your church, about how salvation can be received, but you cannot give it to them. Only God can do that.

The ultimate purpose that we share is to develop and disciple our children in such a way that their faith is strong and their commitment to serve Christ continues into their adult lives. Here are five takeaways that I ask you to consider:

1. *With respect to church institutions, denominational convictions, and parental traditions, look to the Scripture as the ultimate guide.* Go directly to the Bible beginning in Matthew 1:1 and read through the end of Revelation. What does the New Testament teach about baptism? You can see for yourself. It always teaches that salvation precedes baptism. You will not find an example where baptism occurs prior to a person entering a personal faith relationship with Jesus. While it is commendable to dedicate a child to the Lord, each person must personally place his faith in Jesus Christ for salvation and should be instructed to follow that commitment in obedience through baptism.

2. *Encourage obedience in baptism following a personal salvation experience for any and all believers.* At what age should this take place? The Bible does not specify an age but rather specifies an order. The order is salvation followed by baptism. This is appropriate whether eight years of age, eighteen, twenty-eight, fifty-eight, or eighty-eight. The previous chapter was a reminder of caution and wisdom when counseling children regarding salvation. Once it is

clear that your child, a friend, or a fellow church attendee has come to faith in Jesus, encourage them to follow through with public baptism.

3. *Make baptism a memorable experience.* Your church may vary regarding the ceremonial aspect of a baptism service. Within that context, do all you can to make the baptism of your child, friend, or fellow church member a grand celebration. Life is filled with milestones such as graduations, accomplishments, weddings, births, anniversaries, and more. Each is worthy of celebration and recognition. Baptism is a reflection of the most important moment in a person's life. Work with your family and church to make baptism a worthy celebration.

4. *Utilize baptism to share the gospel.* Baptism is not only an act of obedience but is also an opportunity to share God's grace and message of salvation with unbelievers. The symbolism paints a picture that easily translates into a message that encourages others to follow Jesus. Invite as many family and friends as possible to join the celebration when anyone is baptized.

5. *Tell your children your story.* Your story should include what your life was like before coming to know Jesus Christ, how you came to understand that you needed a relationship with Jesus, when, where, and how you trusted Jesus as Savior, and your life since becoming a follower of Jesus. Include the story of your baptism along with why it was a significant part of your faith journey. By the way, that may include being baptized now, as an adult, if you were not baptized following your salvation experience. What a great testimony that would be to your children affirming that you take your faith seriously. Because if you do not, then why should they?

QUESTIONS FOR DISCUSSION

1. What is the teaching and tradition of your church regarding baptism?
2. Based on what you have read, what are some ways you can utilize baptism to strengthen the faith of your children?
3. When were you baptized?
4. What might your church do to make baptism a greater "celebration"?
5. How would you counsel someone who was baptized when young and has no recollection of the experience?

CHAPTER NINE

THERE'S NO PLACE LIKE HOME

Tom Crites

The night my daughter turned one, I reclined in my bed and stared at the ceiling for what seemed like hours reflecting upon the joy of experiencing her first birthday. I remembered how she looked like a Precious Moments doll in her frilly dress with her big beautiful eyes widening while we sang "Happy Birthday." I smiled thinking about how she tentatively touched her cake at first but soon was covered in icing after destroying her piece. I replayed all the adoring comments of our townhouse neighbors who had become our surrogate family since I was attending seminary and we were several hours from home. But both my wife and I knew something, or rather someone, was missing. We missed our parents being there. We were a six-hour drive from her parents and at least a thirteen-hour drive from my hometown, and maybe most burdened by the fact that my dad had died only two years earlier. I wiped away a few tears that evening as I thought about those we were missing.

I like to think that I was in the majority of young people, as I liked visiting home as a young adult. In some ways, it allowed me to feel like a kid again. I could walk in and raid the refrigerator or pantry of all the goodies or kick back on the couch and flip through the channels without any pressing responsibilities. I honestly believe those comfortable feelings stemmed from the fact that I had a good relationship with my parents. But I have visited in the homes of friends where you could cut the tension with a knife. I have heard the late-night confessions of those who loved their parents but could not wait to get away from them. Sometimes I could understand why their relationships were damaged, and other times I silently wondered about the source of all the angst. To me, parents were more than these authoritarian individuals who handed out all the rules and demands. When I landed a role in the spring play, I called my girlfriend and then my mom to share the good news. When my girlfriend broke up with me, I called my dad to get wisdom and prayer. I wanted my parents with me to celebrate my mountaintops and to guide me through my valleys. Yes, they had rules and boundaries, but our relationship flourished within them.

The young adults we surveyed tended to agree. As a matter of fact, for those who grew up attending church, a good relationship with both parents was a very strong indicator that they had stayed in church. As participants shared about their relationships with their mothers, a person who indicated he did not have a close relationship with his mother was 65% more likely to stray from church. A person who did not have a close relationship his father was 50% more likely to stray. Needless to say, relationships within the family are critical to spiritual health.

The Scriptures give us the guide to follow:

> *Children, obey your parents as you would the Lord, because this is right. Honor your father and mother, which is the first commandment with a promise, so that it may go well with you and that you may have a long life in the land. Fathers, don't stir up anger in your children, but bring them up in the training and instruction of the Lord.* (Ephesians 6:1-4 HCSB)

The Apostle Paul reveals the heart of a relationship between parent and child is a relationship to the Lord. He states, "Children obey your parents in the Lord..." and "Fathers, do not stir up anger in your children..." The relationship is reciprocal, but both revolve around a good relationship with the Lord. In other words, children who are in a close relationship with the Lord will honor their parents. Parents who are in a close relationship with the Lord will bring their children up in the right way.

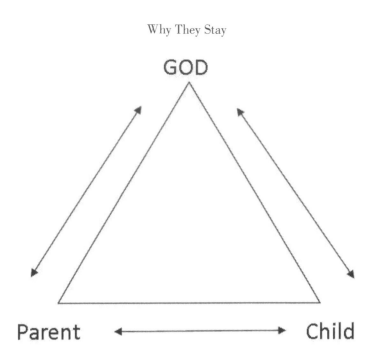

Think of the three points of a triangle: place God at the top angle, parent at the left lower angle, and child at the right lower angle. As the relationship between God and child or God and parent grows closer, the relationship between the parent and child also grows closer. Paul states that if a person is seeking to experience this relationship, thus keeping the fourth commandment, he is promised God's blessings. I believe the blessings that are promised are much more than the temporal blessings of prosperity and long life. They include peace, justice, security, and rest–all given to those entering the Promised Land during the Exodus and given to spiritual travelers today.

Every person needs to be known, accepted, and loved in any relationship. Man tries to satisfy these basic needs from the time he is born until the day he dies. I believe that God created us with these needs to draw us to Him. God has prepared a space in everyone's heart that is only filled by a relationship with Him. He satisfies these needs through salvation. Just think, God knows our deepest, darkest secrets, but He loves us just as we are. He accepts our worthless sinful lives and calls us sons and daughters. He loves us beyond anything we can comprehend. God alone fully satisfies the innate needs of being known, accepted, and loved.

While we are seeking the satisfaction of these needs, God allows man a sneak peek through our godly earthly relationships. As we seek to fulfill these needs in our familial relationships, we get a picture of what God offers in our spiritual relationship with Him. In other words, God allows us to get a taste of a heavenly relationship through the experiences we have with our earthly relationships, especially those with our parents.

It is no coincidence that the number one self-described reason for staying in church was "family upbringing." This identified factor no doubt includes the satisfaction of those basic needs mentioned above. Consider the opportunity a parent has to become that heavenly sneak peek. Parents can know their children better than anyone else until they give them away in marriage. They can accept all the bad habits, failures and defects, and still love them unconditionally. What a great picture of how God loves us. But read the last couple of sentences again–I stated that parents *can* be this for their kids. Unfortunately, many times children are exposed to flaws in the relationship. Parents can damage a child's self-identity with unrealistic expectations, pushing them away by trying to relive a lost childhood, or by pressuring them with unrealistic standards.

I once witnessed a dad do tremendous damage to the relationship with his son over football. The dad had a fantasy of his son playing professional football. He pushed his child so hard toward that goal, but the problem was the boy was only good at football, not great. When the son decided to quit playing football, the dad was frustrated and emotionally beat down his son. In the boy's mind, he was unloved by his father because he did not play football. The damage is still there, and every now and then takes front stage at their family get-togethers. Not only is this young man emotionally scarred, but he also is spiritually damaged. His view of his Heavenly Father is tainted by the experiences he had with his earthly father. The point is that parents have a greater opportunity to influence their child's spiritual development, positively or negatively, more than anyone else in their foundational years. Parents cannot take this responsibility lightly.

The style of discipline utilized by parents can certainly have a profound effect on whether a child of any age feels close to his mom or dad. Developing strong bonds with children deepens as parents play, support, spend time, laugh, develop traditions, and love on their children while providing correction that fosters a growing self-discipline in each child. The correction aspect can be tricky as the parent strives to provide a balanced approach that nurtures and deepens the relationship. Chapter Eleven addresses the issue and relationship of discipline in great detail because the study found that the approach you take can have an impact on the likelihood that your children will stay active in church as adults. Here is the key you must take hold of at this point: understand the importance of a child feeling close to both mom and dad and, therefore, seek to do all in your power to strengthen these relationships.

Children also have some responsibility concerning parent-child relationships; they are an important part of the equation. Remember the illustration? As a child grows closer to the Lord, a relationship with a parent can grow closer, too. The child's relationship to the Lord is just as important as the parents' relationship to the Lord. Face it—we are not perfect. But when we strive to be like Jesus, work toward living our lives close to the Lord, and sincerely try to do God's will, we will improve our earthly relationships.

A Word for Parents

If your children are adults, you may feel that you have failed and that it is too late to make a difference. To tell you the truth, we all have fallen short. I pray that as you read this chapter, God convicted your heart of some things that you need to make right. First, recommit your heart to following God. Make an effort to grow in your faith. Talk with your pastor about how you can become closer to God. Second, I encourage you to work to reconcile your relationships with your children if division has occurred over the years. So many times people avoid the tough conversations because of the emotions that accompany them. Walls built by pride and stubbornness stand in the way of enjoying a growing relationship with your child. I urge you to earnestly try to regain the relationship that you lost. Try simply saying, "I'm sorry." Try writing your apology in a letter if you cannot speak the words. Take the initiative as a parent to repair it. I guarantee that taking one of these steps will not make things worse. It can only make them better.

If you have children still living in your home, you may also feel that you are missing the mark after reading this chapter. Make your relationship with the Lord your number one priority. You will see God's blessings pour over your family. It is a decision you will never regret. One of your most important jobs as a parent is to encourage the spiritual development of your children. It is not to get them in the best schools, the trendiest clothes, or the sportiest cars. Your children do not need you to be their best buddy. They need you to be their godly father or godly mother. Pray for your child's spiritual health. Provide for their spiritual development by being an active part of a local church where they will be taught God's Word. Model spirituality as you seek to follow the Lord.

A Word for Pastors

When you look at your congregation, you can be sure that most every adult there feels like a failure in some area of their lives. Many probably feel like they are failing at their relationships. You have an incredible responsibility to lead your members to find what they are looking for in the Lord. If you have not started small groups where moms and dads can share challenges and encouragements, I recommend that you work to start one as soon as possible. Take inventory of the programs and opportunities that you are offering parents—are they helping to encourage spiritual growth? If not, tweak them to make them worth the time and effort. If you cannot make the necessary adjustments, you may need to cease providing some other good things to focus on the best things for your congregation.

Consider addressing family relationships in your preaching or in a special event. Offer opportunities for family reconciliation in your services. I remember a revival meeting where the evangelist focused on family relationships and called for reconciliation at the end of the service. It was a powerful moment; families all over the room were in tears, holding each other and speaking apologies and words of forgiveness. My family stood in our huddle sharing tears and hugs. It helped break the ice in my fifteen-year-old rebellious heart.

Pastor, do not forsake your family relationships. Remember, your family is not the church. Pastor, your family comes first, then your church. One day you will leave the position of pastor of your current church, but you will always have your family. I have seen the devastation that comes with damaged relationships in a pastor's family. I know what it feels like living in the "glass bubble" as a pastor. I know the pressure of trying to look like the perfect little family. If your members expect you to be that family, they are fooling themselves. Be open and honest with your congregation. Share about your victories and your challenges.

QUESTIONS FOR DISCUSSION

1. What is the status of your relationship with your parents? With each of your children?
2. What were some things that you did as a parent that helped your child feel accepted?
3. How can you help create an environment that will encourage the spiritual development of your child?
4. What can you do this week to start rebuilding a damaged relationship with your child/parent?
5. What can you do to encourage your pastor as he seeks to model healthy family relationships?

CHAPTER TEN

REBEL WITHOUT A CAUSE

Steve Parr

"**M**y wife and I have two wonderful children." *Pause for applause at this point.* "And we also have a third child!" Those were the words of a comedian I recently heard as he launched into a segment of his routine. If you have more than one child you may relate to his sentiment. I happen to have three children, and they are all wonderful; however, they are not the same. Quite frankly, one of them really tested my wife and me as parents with a rebellious streak that caused several years of tremendous emotional angst. I am not complaining, and I want to begin first by telling you how she turned out as an adult. She is awesome. She is a gracious young lady, married, with a great work ethic, good with managing finances, caring, and as good of a daughter as a parent could wish for. During her adolescent years, she never made me curse... (But as an old country boy might say) if someone had written it down, I would have likely signed it.

Getting a grip on discipline with my rebellious strong-willed daughter was a great mystery during her adolescent years. We managed it pretty well when she was a child, although we could see the seeds of the challenges early on. I tried reason, conversation, logic, grounding, screaming, weeping, trying to heap some guilt on her, giving freedom, taking away all freedom, and then I tried to think of other options for the following weekend. She was a mess.

I am not going to get into all that she got into, but I was scared. I feared for her and her future because of the path that she was on. This situation took place over the course of several years. She was our very strong-willed child. We did get through it, and the story has a positive ending, but that is not always the case.

My other two daughters would be considered compliant. One is somewhat compliant and the other is very compliant. Let me give you an actual scenario and follow by distinguishing some of the qualities of compliant and strong-willed children. I arrived home on a Sunday night to discover my high school daughter sitting in the dining room, with no television or electronic devices to distract her, studying. I did not say she was cramming for an exam or rushing at the last minute to beat a deadline for an assignment. No. She was just studying with no prompting from her mother or me. Are you kidding me?

I never studied on a Sunday in my whole life as a student, and I certainly did not have the discipline to just take time on a weekend evening to stay caught up. You recall the challenges I mentioned with one of my other daughters? With this young lady, though I have corrected and rebuked her, she has never been grounded, never have I had to raise my voice, and she has never been in serious trouble. That is not to say that she has not been involved in mischief, and I am wise enough to know that she has probably gotten away with a few things. I know this from experience as a compliant child myself. Everyone tests boundaries on some level even if they appear compliant. However, she makes me look like the parent of the year with her sweet disposition, self-discipline, and good behavior.

What did I do different as a parent with these two that made them so different? The answer is...nothing. They were born with different natures. We asked the young adults we surveyed about their nature growing up. Were they very compliant, somewhat compliant, somewhat strong-willed, or very strong-willed? Interestingly the answers almost fell into equal quarters.

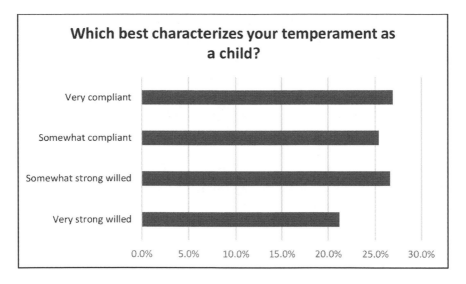

Let us consider in general terms the differences between the compliant and the strong-willed child in order to understand the effect that their nature might have on the probability that they will stray or stay in church as adults. The compliant child will test boundaries but quickly draw back if challenged by someone in authority. They tend to follow the rules, avoid major confrontations, and appear to have a natural self-discipline that emerges early on, although with boys it is usually delayed until later adolescence or young adulthood. They are generally easy to parent, and as I stated earlier, are not immune to mischief, but they tend to avoid extremes and steer clear of most unhealthy types of behavior.

The strong-willed child, on the other hand, believes he or she is in charge. Before he can put together a full sentence, he learns to manipulate to get his way and seeks to master the skill as he grows. He lives to test the boundaries and appears to take joy in stepping over the line. He sees discipline as a simple inconvenience and does not hesitate to go right back to and beyond the behavior for which he was disciplined. He lives for debate, does not mind confrontation, and may not respond to all types of discipline. Bear in mind that these are generalizations to give you a broad view of the differences.

I heard a popular Christian psychologist describe a family with four daughters. They were the model family with perfectly behaved, prim and proper girls. Other adults admired and envied these parents for their child-rearing skills. Then the parents got a late surprise. Child number five came into their life, and it happened to be a little boy. What others did not realize up to this point is that although these were good parents, all four of the girls were compliant. Not so for the little boy. He was very strong-willed. These model parents then went on a wild ride and discovered that you can be a great mom or dad and still have your hands full if you have a strong-willed child. The challenge they encountered was not because they had a boy, and it was not because he was born later in their marriage. He was very strong-willed and in that case would have been a challenge to any parent.

Here is how my family breaks down. My wife would have been very compliant as a child in my estimation. I was somewhat compliant. I never gave my parents any problems, and though I tested boundaries and got into mischief, I always tended to quickly move back within the borders of expectation. Of my three daughters, one is very strong-willed, one is somewhat compliant, and one is very compliant. We did not raise them any differently, but they were not the same. Growing up as a compliant child and having a wife that was likewise compliant resulted in a complication when we had a strong-willed child. We did not know, at the outset, how to parent her, especially during adolescence. We learned and got a grip on it through much turmoil and struggle, including seeking out professional counsel. Based on what you have learned about my family, I want to ask you a question. We raised our girls in the church and always tried to model the Christian faith in our home. All three of our daughters are young adults. Two are in church and one is not. Which one do you think most likely strayed from church?

If you guessed that it was the very strong-willed child, you would be correct. I want to pause here since I am getting personal to add a bit more context. My daughter who is not currently in church has a solid moral character. She made a commitment to follow Christ when she was young, was baptized, and grew up attending church. She is not antagonistic toward church and is not averse to attending upon personal invitations. She is spiritual and states that she intends to raise her children in church. With her permission, I am being transparent to help you understand some of the dynamics that cause young adults to stay in church or to stray from church. I am blessed in this regard because many of you can tell the story of a strong-willed child who has rejected the church as an adult, rejected their family's values, and is antagonistic towards spiritual things. However, be cautious about making judgments about families who love and serve the Lord, yet have a child who has strayed.

As a matter of fact, our study revealed that there was little or no variation between whether a young adult had stayed in church or strayed if they viewed their temperament while growing up as very compliant, somewhat compliant, or somewhat strong-willed. However, we discovered that a very strong-willed child was 42.5% more likely to have strayed from church as a young adult than to have stayed, and the variation is significantly larger than with the other three groups.

Likewise, when you consider those who were very compliant and somewhat compliant contrasted with the somewhat strong-willed and the very strong-willed, you see a significant difference in the likelihood of straying if the child had more of a rebellious nature. This factor may be the most challenging for us to address since we have no control over the temperament of a child. However, there is action that we can take.

Consider this positive takeaway before reading further. Not all strong-willed children end up straying. You may recall the guiding principle from Chapter Five about probabilities. Awareness of the probability is important, and to use a cliché, knowledge is power. If you have a strong-willed child, the other fourteen points in this section should be studied and applied with greater fervency to counter the challenge faced by the nature of the strong-willed child. You can be victorious as a parent. You can also be very empathetic with parents who face the same challenges that you are well acquainted with.

A Word for Parents

You are reading an important chapter. You should be encouraged because you may have been pulling your hair out wondering what you have done wrong, when in reality the challenges you are facing are rooted in the temperament your child was born with. You can take solace on one hand that not all of the issues you face are related to your parenting skills. On the other hand, you do have a responsibility. You cannot wash your hands of the responsibility to do anything and everything possible to guide your strong-willed child in the right direction. Begin by understanding your child and mentally noting where he fits in this spectrum. If you have a very compliant child he will make you look like a great parent much as an all-star athlete can make even a mediocre coach look great. As the parent of a strong-willed child, I want to give you some thoughts that may help:

1. *Become a student of parenting.* The parents of compliant children do not need seminars or books. They still have work to do but you, as a parent of a strong-willed child, are going to have to work overtime. Read books (plural) about parenting strong-willed children, and the sooner you begin the better— but it is never too late. I read a book when my daughter was a teen called *The Hurting Parent* by Gregg and Margie Lewis that addressed this issue and helped me to grow in my skills tremendously.

2. *Reflect on your own temperament.* If you and your spouse were compliant as children, then the task is going to be more challenging for you. Parents who were strong-willed themselves will better understand and be more immune to the manipulative nature of the rebellious child. I struggled because I did not think like my child was thinking. It was not my nature. Godly counsel is important no matter where you stand, but I encourage you to get counsel and coaching from a strong Christian adult who himself was a strong-willed child.

3. *Back up but don't back down.* You may have to eat some crow at this point. Do you remember when you said, "I will never allow my child to..." You will have to identify some safe areas to give room for your child to express some degree of rebellion that is not unhealthy, although you thought you would never allow it. I never gave my children an option about whether to go to church. I have a responsibility for their spiritual nurture, and staying connected to a local body of believers is biblical and spiritually healthy. However, I did allow for some wiggle room on the schedule and where they would attend as they got older.

This was especially important for my strong-willed child. If I said black, she said white. If I said up, she said down. If I said tall, she said short. So, if I said this church, her nature was to say no church. Since that was not an option, I suggested, if not this church then choose another church so long as you go. I gave some liberty about where she would attend and frequency of attendance during the week, but not *if* she would attend somewhere each week. I backed up but I never backed down.

4. *Win the early battles.* If you are not winning the battles when they are two years old then you are in serious trouble when they turn thirteen. Mark Twain suggested that once a child turns thirteen, you should place him in a barrel, nail the lid shut, and feed him through the knot hole. Twain went on to say that when the child turns sixteen, you should plug the knot hole! I am not so pessimistic about teens, but this I know: you must let your child know from the outset what authority is. I am sure you are familiar with the term "spoiled brat." It is the child who rarely or never hears the word "no" from the parent. You are the parent. You are the authority. Do not give in to crying, whining, or complaining when they are infants lest they learn early on that you can be manipulated. No child ever perished from crying. See that you meet their needs and attend to their safety, but they do not have to get their way. Your responsibility is not to make your child happy but to help them to mature and be healthy. Be the parent! You can be their friend after they finish college.

5. *Don't be discouraged when you get discouraged.* It is going to happen. You are going to struggle, the children will get in trouble, you are going to be embarrassed, they are going to scare you to death, and with all of that, you are going to get through it. I was blessed to have a loving spouse and we were able to encourage one another. If you are a single parent, you have an admitted disadvantage because a strong-willed child can wear you down. You need someone to keep you propped up when you are discouraged to help you make wise parenting decisions. Therefore, it is so important that you connect with a person or a group that you can meet with

regularly who can cheer you on, counsel you, and help you to stay on the right course.

It is so sad to see parents who give up when their children are only thirteen, fourteen, or fifteen and allow them to do what they want as if neglecting the challenges will make the problems go away. You have work to do and it will not be complete as long as they are teens. The other side of that is there will be a point where you do let them go and must give them over to the Lord. That is scary. What about when they are nineteen, twenty, or twenty-one? They should not be living in your basement, not working, not in school, or bringing things into your home that you do not approve of. Do not get so discouraged that you give in and let them make the decisions that you are responsible for. Do not turn into an enabler. They must learn to stand on their own. Work together with your spouse and/or with other godly parents to give you counsel. Most importantly, stay close to God. If you have a strong-willed child, trust me, you will need it!

A Word for Pastors

I hope the wheels of your brain are already turning. You need to preach on this subject to encourage and equip parents. You can also foster understanding since parents of compliant children may be prone to judge those with strong-willed children as less capable when, in fact, God gave them a strong-willed child. Upon reflection, I am honored that God thought me worthy of raising a strong-willed child, and I am most grateful for what God taught me through the experience. I love my daughter unconditionally and always did, even amid the deepest parts of our struggles when she was younger. God did that through me because he loves us in spite of the fact that we sin by nature and by choice.

I also hope you will preach specifically about parenting to give your parishioners insight and tools to be more effective. Our aim is to assist parents to make disciples of their children that will serve Jesus throughout their lives. In addition, preach to teens and children helping them to understand themselves as well as their responsibilities to their parents and to God.

One last thought for you to consider as a pastor: is your church open to strong-willed teens? They will misbehave, sometimes create problems, and perhaps tear things up. I am sure the Gadarene Demoniac is grateful that Jesus reached out to him in spite of his problems. Is your church reaching out? Once again, that person who grew up with a rebellious spirit may be just the person who can relate to those teens. Remember that children and teens with this nature will not do well by sitting still, listening to lectures, and being asked not to talk. You will not likely impress them with customary traditional methods that are common to the typical church. God loves them, and we should also. Take time to identify children and teens that are strong-willed and ask them how your church can do better at meeting their needs.

One Final Word to Adults Who Grew Up Strong-Willed

Perhaps this chapter is about you. Someone may have asked you to read it as a reflection understanding your temperament and the challenges you personally faced growing up. You have always had somewhat of a rebellious streak and often found it difficult if not impossible to comply. Now you are an adult. What now?

God created you the way that you are. Consider this, however: he did not give you the nature that you have ultimately to cause separation. You have experiences and abilities that your journey has provided that would not have been possible apart from your strong-willed nature. Perhaps you have fought with addiction. If so, you are uniquely equipped to help others who are experiencing similar struggles. Perhaps you are now a parent yourself. You will be an excellent resource to guide and encourage parents who have strong-willed children.

Here is the bottom line. You are an adult now. You are responsible and you cannot blame your raising or your temperament for where you are at this point. You are accountable to God and need to make a personal response. God loves you and desires to bless you in a special way. You may have struggled with spiritual commitment though your parents tried to teach you the right way to go. At this point it is not about your parents. It is about you and God. In spite of your natural inclination to resist submission, I challenge you to give your life over to Jesus Christ and allow Him to use you to make a difference in the lives of others. You will be surprised at the freedom you can experience by submitting your life to the leadership of the Lord Jesus Christ.

QUESTIONS FOR DISCUSSION

1. How would you describe your temperament as a child? What are the strengths and weaknesses of that temperament in the way it has shaped you?
2. If you have children, describe their temperaments.
3. What would you add to the list of advice for parents of strong-willed children?
4. Do you know an adult who was strong-willed as a child and has strayed from church? How might what you learned in this chapter help you in ministering and witnessing to them?
5. How might your church do a better job of equipping parents?
6. How might your church be more effective in engaging strong-willed children and teens?

CHAPTER ELEVEN

YOU ARE GROUNDED

Tom Crites

"Ding, ding, ding," the small bell echoed through the arena as the announcer stepped up to the microphone. "It is time for the main event... let's get ready to rumm–bulll!" The words stretched out for effect, rousing the anticipation of a blood-and-guts battle. "In this corner, mom and dad, and in this corner, (the music starts to build creating an emotional buzz) the undisputed light-weight champion of her world... baby!" The announcer dropped the microphone and the referee stepped forward, "I want an unfair fight. Baby, you scream, bite, claw, kick, hit, yell, fall on the floor, screech, and become like a wet piece of spaghetti in your parents' grasp. Parents, I want you to pull your hair out. Let's fight!"

Can you relate? There is not a mom or dad in the world who has not struggled with the day-to-day challenges of being a parent. At times, parenting can be an excruciating and painful experience while, at other times, a glimpse of heaven. Raising a child can be both one of the most difficult and yet most rewarding experiences of one's life. I have two great kids. Both are now in their twenties and the baby battle days are long past, but I can remember them like they were yesterday. My wife and I read every parenting book we could find, talked to our parents, talked to our pediatrician, compared notes with our friends with children, and prayed our way through the formative years of our own kids. We lost many of those baby battles, but we won enough to see our kids turn out okay.

In our study, young adults were asked about the factors that contributed to their staying in church, and many shared that their parents' style of discipline may have contributed significantly to their spiritual state. Participants were asked to describe the disciplinary style they experienced in their home and were given a scale that offered several choices ranging from "abusive" to "very loose." It was interesting to see that the experiences were diverse and spread across the scale, including both "abusive" and "very loose" extremes. Young adults who have stayed plugged into church indicated that their parents had a more "balanced" disciplinary style than those who strayed from church. A person who grew up in a "somewhat strict" environment was 21% more likely to stray, and as the disciplinary style moved to "very strict" and eventually to "abusive," the percentages of young adults straying from church increased more precipitously.

It is clear: parents bear responsibility for providing discipline for their children as they raise them with the goal of nurturing a developing self-discipline within each child. The nature of discipline naturally invokes tension between the parent and child on many occasions. Development of a clear understanding of the difference between punishment and discipline is critical. Punishment can be a great motivator for behavioral change but can severely damage a relationship, as invoking pain on some level is central to punishment. Discipline, on the other hand, is an action that is conducted to correct behavior but is done in the interest of correction rather than harm. Punishment will serve to drive a wedge between a parent and a child. Failure to address improper behavior will fail to foster the necessary self-discipline that a child needs to develop and embrace.

I remember the anxiety I faced as my kids were coming into the world. Things seemed so evil. I saw the influence of a liberal culture as drug and alcohol abuse became mainstream, sexual recklessness became the norm, and biblical principles were questioned. I think about the parents today who are facing a world that seems completely upside-down with the legalization and legitimizing of sinful acts and lifestyles. In the United States, people are taught to tolerate everything except a Christian worldview. It seems like our culture could not get any more immoral. Raising a child in this context can be terrifying! Only an unwise person would try to raise a child in this world apart from God. I am so thankful that God helped me traverse the child-raising years. I am confident that He will help you, too! We can thank God that His Word is timeless and His reach limitless. He never changes and His principles stand forever. Let's consider His Word as it relates to parenting in today's world.

I am so thankful that God offers me help as a parent in His Scriptures. Many times throughout the Bible we are called God's children, and He is the perfect Father. I think Hebrews 12:7-8 applies directly to this issue: *Endure suffering as discipline: God is dealing with you as sons. For what son is there that a father does not discipline? But if you are without discipline—which all receive— then you are illegitimate children and not sons.* (HCSB) In verses 10 and 11, the writer tells us why God disciplines His children: *For they disciplined us for a short time based on what seemed good to them, but He does it for our benefit, so that we can share in His holiness. No discipline seems enjoyable at the time, put painful. Later on, however, it yields the fruit of peace and righteousness to those who have been trained by it.* (HCSB) God disciplines His children because He loves them. This is our example, and we can demonstrate our love for our children through a balanced approach to discipline.

Chip Ingram, with Living on the Edge, wrote a helpful guide to balanced discipline, which is actually biblical discipline.[27] I was able to glean much from his experience as a dad. He helps us understand that God uses discipline to help His children avoid destruction. As parents, we have had the chance to live and make mistakes. We have learned the meanings of right and wrong. We have felt heartache and success. Through these experiences we can help guide our children as they navigate through life. Think about it this way: when my children were little, I told them to stay in our yard while playing. I did not want them to play in the street because I knew that there was a chance they could get run over by an oncoming car. I set boundaries for them out of love. I wanted to keep them from harm. If they did venture into the street, I would yell their name and scold them. At the time it was painful for them to have their father yell at them or make them sit in time-out for a couple of minutes. But

I knew that the pain they were experiencing in that moment might prevent them from tremendous pain in the future. My intent was not to keep them from having fun, but rather to protect them from harm because of my love for them.

Much in the same way, God disciplines to express His love. The fact that He even notices me is a tremendous act of grace but, even more, that He cares about me is an expression of His love. Proverbs 3:11-12 says, "My son, do not despise the Lord's discipline and do not resent His rebuke, because the Lord disciplines those He loves, as a father the son delights in." (NIV) You want evidence that God loves you? You have it in His discipline. He has given His instructions to guide us. The word that is translated "discipline" in verse 11 is the Hebrew word *musar,* which means instruction. I am notorious for not following the instructions. My wife calls it the "Crites way of doing it." My brother and I scoff at instructions when they come in a package: "We don't need any stinkin' instructions!" we boast. But after about an hour or two of wrestling with the toy or piece of furniture, I whisper, "Where are those instructions?" God has given us His instructions for life because He loves us. We must never set His instructions aside. A wise person will heed God's Word and try to do His will.

God also gives us correction. The other word translated "discipline" in that Proverbs 3: 11-12 passage is the Hebrew word *yakah.* It means reproof or correction. So, we see that God offers His instructions before and His corrections after. God's discipline describes the boundaries of my "safe zone." There, I can bring honor to His name (Proverbs 1:9), receive wisdom (Proverbs 8:33), avoid poverty and shame (Proverbs 13:18), obtain favor (Proverbs 8:35), and find real life (Proverbs 4:13). God measured out His boundaries for my spiritual benefit in His instruction and He keeps me inside those boundaries through His correction. He does not seek to punish me, but as a loving Father provides the correction that I need. The correction can be painful, but it is received differently because I know it flows from His love.

A balanced disciplinary style will include both instruction and correction. Both of these must be balanced with love in the right attitude or they become control and punishment. Look at the chart on the next page to understand what happens when a parent is out-of-balance.

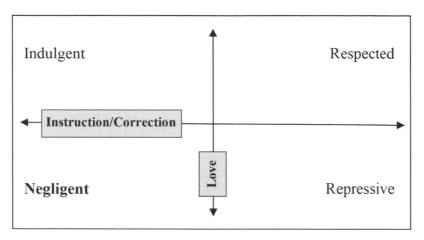

The first type of out-of-balance parent is the most tragic of all the types, the **Negligent Parent.** A parent of this type offers little or no instruction or correction and demonstrates very little love toward his or her child. In many cases a negligent parent is dealing with issues that impair his or her reasoning. Many times, parents who find themselves in this destructive place are victims of their own negligent parents. The issues could be related to past relationships causing emotional and mental illness. The issues may include drug or alcohol abuse which inhibits a parent's ability to function normally. If the parent does not experience the intervention of a pastor, teacher, social worker, or relative, the cycle of tragedy can be expected to be transferred to another generation. This is a very damaging context and unfortunately there are thousands of children existing in this situation in our neighborhoods right under the shadows of our steeples. Children who grow up in homes that are negligent develop deep emotional scars. Children can break the cycle of negligence through the love of Jesus and the help of a caring group of believers in a local church. Interventions may be required to minister to a child who the Lord brings into your life.

The second type of out-of-balance parent is the **Indulgent Parent**. A child of this type of parent will perceive that he has little instruction and correction but lots of love. The parent is very tolerant of the child's behavior and generally allows the child to have whatever he or she wants.

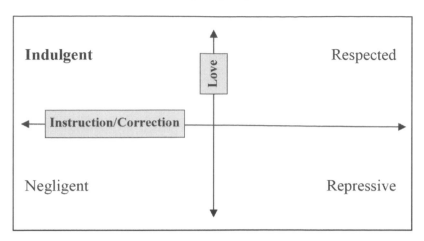

Boundaries are not evident or are very loose at best. A parent who is indulgent may warn that the child is going to be corrected but seldom follows through with the correction or the severity of the correction. Parents lose the respect of their children as the inconsistencies build. An indulgent parent has a desire to become his or her child's best friend, but that is seldom—if ever—realized. Children come to the conclusion that their parents exist in their world for the satisfaction of their desires. A child of an indulgent parent will likely become insecure due to the lack of boundaries in his or her childhood. As young adults, these individuals are faced with moral dilemma after moral dilemma as they try to navigate through the real world without clear boundaries of right and wrong.

Repressive: The out-of-balance parent operating in this style has clearly defined the boundaries through lots of instruction and correction but finds it difficult or does not desire to express love toward the child. "Because I said so," is the mantra of this parent. Obedience is expected and enforced. Parents in this home may be light on the instruction and heavy on the correction. Children who grow up in this type of home tend to be rebellious.

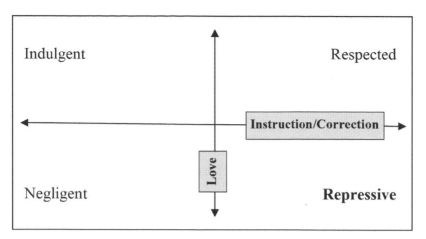

They have spent their teenage years fighting with their parents and cannot wait to get out of the house. They spend their young adult years reestablishing the boundaries on their own terms and trying to understand the "whys" of those boundaries.

The final type of parenting could be called **Respected.** This parent is compassionate yet firm when setting boundaries for their child. They have clear instruction and fair, consistent corrections. They have balanced the instruction and correction with love, identifying the "safety zone" which is acceptable and encouraged. This type of parenting is balanced parenting.

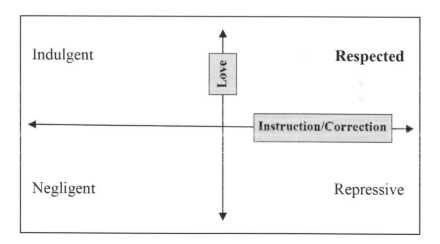

Since I have mentioned that the keys to a balanced parenting style are clear instruction and fair, consistent corrections balanced by love, let's look a bit deeper at what that might look like in a family context. First, parents who are attempting to be balanced offer clear expectations. Children in a balanced home understand the spiritual limits of a believer through the parent's example and the influence of their church. These children know that they have specific physical responsibilities related to the functions of the family. The children learn that they are not allowed to bite the neighbor or hit their brother. These children may have a few chores that they are to complete regularly which may include cleaning their room, taking out the trash, or helping with a sibling. They see that they are an important part of the family and they have a place to fit in. They understand the emotional place that they live in. Their parents have demonstrated and told them that they are loved and that their love is also accepted and wanted. These children learn that they are an important part of their family. The instruction that they receive is biblically-based and steady.

On the other side of instruction is correction. I remember a moment when my daughter was sixteen. She had a car that we provided to get her and her brother to school. One day, we unexpectedly arrived early at one of her afterschool band practices and found her car missing. We assumed she had to run a quick errand before the end of practice and decided to wait for her return. We were surprised to see two of her friends arrive in her car without her. Since we had discussed the rules regarding her car, she knew immediately that she was in "big time trouble." The moment was not fun: she was embarrassed, and I was disappointed and a bit angry. We talked about the issue, I took her keys for a while (which she did not appreciate at all) and she learned that we were serious about the boundary that we had set. As far as I know, she did not let a friend drive her car again without my permission.

Correction is an important part of balanced discipline. After the limits are set, then correction takes place if the limits are compromised. A child should understand the instruction and how he did not meet the expectation, and then be directed to correct the problem. If the parent ignores the need for correction, the child will learn that the boundary is not "real" and will, therefore, search to find the "real" boundary. Understand, the child will not like correction; it is against his nature. But it is critical that the child experience correction to learn the boundaries. It is important to note the fact that young adults who have stayed in church indicated that their parents had a more "balanced" disciplinary style than those who strayed from church.

A Word for Parents

If you are like every other parent in the world, you realize that you made some mistakes trying to raise your kids. Unfortunately, time machines have not been invented yet and we cannot go back and redo those times when we blew it. You can start from where you are, and if your children are still in your home it is not too late. The older they are, the more difficult it will be to make changes and you may need to get help from others who have some expertise. Do not shy away from admitting your shortcomings to your children and stating that you are resetting your approach to parenting. If you have been overly strict, your children will likely be thrilled. If you have been too lenient, they may not be happy with your decision. Their long-term health is what is most important rather than their current happiness. Do what is right and begin now.

Acknowledging your own shortcomings and commitment to be a better parent will help your children understand you better. It will be another chance for them to hear how much you love them. You may have adult children now, or teens trying to spread their wings. You might still be wiping noses and changing diapers. Whatever your circumstances, it is never too early or late to communicate your love to your children. Take time to tell your kids how much you love them and how much you want the best for them. You will not regret it.

Every parent needs to take advantage of the wisdom and opportunity that comes with being a part of a parenting community. Get involved with a local church where you can meet and share life with other parents. Find a family member or friend who is a veteran parent—one who has been through the baby battles—who can give you advice and Godly counsel. Be open and honest about your struggles and challenges. Realize that no one expects for you to have a perfect child and no one expects you to be the perfect parent, except you. Take advantage of the support community that God has placed in your life.

A Word for Pastors

What is your church doing to help parents do a better job of raising their children in a balanced way that honors God? Consider gathering a group of parents to brainstorm together about ways that your ministry can have a more positive impact. Bring in specialists and share your own stories and struggles. Do not neglect to share what God's Word teaches about parenting without apology. Even your struggles can be an encouragement to others because all parents struggle unless they have a house full of very compliant children.

You may want to identify a good veteran couple in your church–a couple that has been through the battles–and challenge them to develop a ministry to parents. Offer opportunities for the parents in your church to share and grow through biblically-based parenting classes. Build a resource list naming books, speakers, courses, and other helpful tools to equip your parents. You could also consider seminars, retreats, sermon series, and guest experts to help your parents do a better job. Almost every parent needs a boost and all need to be encouraged. Take leadership in this matter because it may be the difference in whether many of the children in your church are still attending when they become adults.

QUESTIONS FOR DISCUSSION

1. As a parent: what is (or was) the greatest challenge for you in practicing a balanced approach to discipline?
2. What is the most helpful resource you have discovered in helping you to understand biblical parenting and balanced discipline?
3. As a church: what can you do to assist the parents in your community in becoming balanced discipline parents?

CHAPTER TWELVE

DADDY, DO YOU LOVE MAMMA?

Steve Parr

"Your mom and I are splitting up." I was in utter shock when I heard these words. Perhaps I was naïve. Maybe I was ignoring the signs. It could be that my parents hid their troubles from my sister and me very well. I felt as if someone had punched me right in the stomach and that was just the beginning of what seemed to be unending months of emotional pain. My mom and dad were the best parents in the world. No one could have asked for a better upbringing than they provided with a beautiful balance of love, discipline, fun times, and instruction.

I was twenty-six years of age when my father came to my home to have this serious conversation. Although he justified the decision and portrayed an acceptance of this change of direction, I took the news very hard. Reflecting on those days I understand now that my parents meant me no harm when they made the decision and that my sister and I were in no way the cause of their problems. However, when you are in the midst of the storm it is difficult to interpret everything correctly. To make matters worse the confidence that he displayed in his initial conversation with me was not well founded. Divorce is rarely amicable, and some difficult days ensued where I found myself torn and often in the middle of my parents' marital and post-marital difficulties.

I want to express something that is very important as we consider this next issue. There is no condemnation in what I am about to share. Not for my parents, not for those who have experienced the pain of divorce, and not for you if that has been a part of your life's journey. The subject that we are considering is what compels those who grow up in church to stay in church once they become adults. We cannot ignore that a significant issue was uncovered and should consider any adjustments that might be made that will enhance the probability that today's children and teens will grow in faith and serve Jesus as adults.

Degrees of pain are difficult if not impossible to compare. Everyone experiences disappointments, crises, tragedies, hurts, and emotional trauma on many occasions and on multiple levels. Jesus reminded His followers, *"You will have suffering in this world." (John 16:33 HCSB)* Christians are not immune to difficulty and pain. Jesus said that, *"He [God] causes His sun to rise on the evil and the good, and sends rain on the righteous and the unrighteous."* (Matthew 5:45 HCSB) However, when you look at scales that rate the degree of stress from those who serve in the fields of psychology and human behavior, you will always find the pain associated with divorce near the very top. As an example, the *Holmes and Rahe Stress Scale* rates divorce second, only behind the death of a spouse.[28] The trauma runs deep and the effects are not limited to the couple going through the process. I learned this first-hand with my experience.

I often wondered how I would have handled the news and the subsequent storm that ensued had I been a child or a teenager. By the age of twenty-six my faith was deeply rooted, growing, and I was new to the call to ministry. In addition, I was blessed to have a spouse that gave me support and nurture during the darkest points of my experience. But what happens to a child with more shallow roots of faith because they are young? What happens if no personal faith has been initiated? What happens where there is no relationship with the depth of a strong marriage to provide support? Though mom and dad can say what sounds like the right words and try to give assurance that all will be well, the storm will ordinarily continue and the hurts are not easily erased. That pain includes a spiritual consequence for many who experience the divorce of their parents.

The study revealed that a young adult (age 26-39) with divorced parents was 11.6% more likely to have strayed from church than one whose parents were still married. We all know of people who have experienced trauma in their lives that caused them to question the value of faith, God's love, or even the existence of God. That did not happen to me because my faith had been developing and growing over the previous thirteen years. The consequences are astonishing when you consider the impact on those who experience the divorce of parents as teenagers. Adolescents are already vulnerable as they are framing their worldview, testing boundaries, wrestling with questions, and going through a physical hormonal storm. When divorce is added to that equation the results can be spiritually devastating. If divorce occurs during high school or later, he or she is 100% or twice as likely to stray from church as the child who goes through the experience prior to age eleven.

A Word for Parents

Let's briefly address three groups at this point to see how we might minimize or eliminate, where possible, this issue as a factor in the growth of our children as disciples of Jesus Christ. The three groups are those parents who have experienced divorce, those who are contemplating divorce, and those who currently have strong marriages.

First, for those who have experienced divorce: be assured again that there is no condemnation intended. The assumption is that you cannot turn back the clock nor can you undo what has been done as far as the former marriage is concerned. Whether you were the victim, an equal contributor, or the cause of the divorce, the dynamics are not always simple and the application is likely more complex than the advice. What do you do now (if you have not already done so)?

1. *Do all you can to avoid undermining the respect your child(ren) has for your former spouse.* You would do well to go back and re-read Chapter Nine at this point. Those young adults who stay in church say that they had a close relationship to **both** their mom and their dad growing up. The key word here is "both." You need to facilitate and nurture the relationship between your child(ren) and your former spouse to the greatest degree possible. Please avoid the temptation

to use your child(ren) as a weapon or a tool. You are making a disciple and that responsibility is not absolved by a divorce.

2. *In cooperation with your former spouse, stay engaged with your children.* They need your love, assurance, attention, and support in an even greater way than when you were married. Occasional visits will not suffice. The child needs a close relationship with both mom and dad if possible. Though the marriage is dissolved, the partnership must actually grow as parents, and step-parents, cooperatively work together to minimize instability, provide support, and give the children the tools they need to mature both spiritually as well as practically. A contentious separation no doubt makes this a challenge. Commit to take the high road at all points and in all matters, seeking to provide in partnership with the other parent(s) the best possible situation for the healthy development of your child(ren) under the circumstances.

3. *Continue to practice and grow in your faith.* Do you want a sure way to sabotage the faith of your child(ren)? Here is how: go through a contentious divorce, disconnect one of the parents from the child(ren), and stop going to church. The likelihood of those children serving the Lord as adults is very low and is the exception more than the rule. You cannot change what happened in the past, but you can begin to move in the best possible direction beginning today.

4. *Get help for your children.* They have had a traumatic experience, and it is greater if they were in their adolescence. Provide them with the resources, professional counsel, and support needed to strengthen their faith and get them through the challenges the crisis contributes to the development of their faith.

Second, for those parents who are contemplating divorce; the situation in which you find yourself is likely complex and some circumstances may be beyond your control. However, to the degree that you can have influence, here are some words of wisdom.

1. *Allow the potential spiritual consequences to your children to motivate you to reconciliation and a healthier marriage.*

You still have time. It may take a miracle or it may be that you have simply contemplated divorce with no specific actions yet taken. You must ask the question, "Which is more important at this point?" It will be difficult because it will call for a major sacrifice on your part. Which is of the greatest necessity, your happiness or your children's spiritual health? If they are in high school, the spiritual damage caused is almost ten times as devastating. The suggestion is not simply that you hang on and bear with it, although that may be necessary. The exhortation is to recommit to do all you can to have a healthy marriage.

2. *Do not put the burden on your children.* Be reminded that neither children nor teens are emotionally mature enough to provide you with counsel. Refer to Chapter Nine and to the previous counsel for those who have experienced divorce. It is important that children and teens have a strong relationship to both mom and dad. Though you may be right in your opinions and justified in your concerns about your spouse, you do your children no spiritual favors by undermining your spouse through criticism or debate for which you expect your child to make judgments. Do not put that responsibility on them. You should certainly seek Godly counsel, but not from your children on issues related to marital difficulties.

3. *Attend to your spiritual development.* How is your devotional life right now? Are you reading God's Word every day? You should be. You should be engaging His Word so that you can grow, glean wisdom, make good decisions, and model spiritual growth for your children. Are they seeing it? The temptation is to back away from practicing spiritual disciplines, attending church, and seeking to serve others when you are in the midst of crisis. Ironically, that is often when it is most important for the one admittedly contemplating divorce.

4. *Do not give up.* Adolescence is filled with enough drama and trauma even when mom and dad love each other and have a great relationship. Recommit to resolving and rekindling what started as a love strongly rooted. Your reconciliation can serve as an example to your children of the same sacrificial

and unconditional love that exemplifies the love of Jesus Christ. You certainly should not compromise the physical safety of your children or yourself in pursuit of this aim.

Third, for those who currently have strong marriages; I am happy to say that the divorce of my parents motivated me. It actually made my marriage stronger. I committed, not only for the sake of my children, but for the joy that a happy marriage brings, to constantly work to have a good marital relationship. I think I can speak to this with integrity since I have been blessed to be happily married for thirty-five years. I am not better than anyone else and I know some wonderful people who have experienced divorce.

One of the greatest things you can do to enhance the spiritual development of your children is to love their mom (or dad if you are the wife). I have found that my spiritual growth strengthens my marriage. I am blessed to have a godly wife who loves the Lord. I have never done anything to discourage her from growing spiritually and serving the Lord. However, as a pastor, I have seen men (not to say a wife could not likewise be guilty) get upset at the frequency of his wife's church attendance or her service to the church or community. Why? I want my wife to love and serve the Lord because that appears to make her love me even more. I do not know about you but I need all the help I can get. Attend to your personal spiritual development and recommit to love your spouse and model a healthy marriage for your children. They are much more likely to be serving Jesus Christ as adults when this is done.

A Word for Pastors

1. *Begin in your own home.* How is your marriage going? Are you still dating your wife, spending time with the family, loving your wife as Christ loves the church? Your members need to be encouraged, and one of the ways you can do so is to begin with your own marriage. You know by now that being a pastor does not automatically or mystically make everything right at home. You have to work at it like everyone else. Remember, if you lose your family, you will likely lose your ministry. Therefore, which should be your priority?

Your church or your family? You did not marry the church. You married your wife. Go home and love on her!

2. *Preach it!* When is the last time you preached messages to strengthen the relationships between husbands and wives, parents and children? God's Word is filled with exhortation and you should not neglect to teach and preach what the Bible says about the keys to these relationships. Perhaps the principles of this chapter can enhance your exposition as you encourage healthier marriages.

3. *Be empathetic.* Many who have experienced divorce will tell you that church attendance can be difficult. Striking the balance between affirming healthy marriages and ministering to those wounded by divorce is not simple. If that were so, every church would have a handle on it. How is it going in your congregation? Are you affirming healthy marriages while providing healing for those who have been hurt by broken marriages? Perhaps you need to have a conversation with some of your leaders to improve on this.

The Rest of the Story

I will not get into all that occurred the two years following the conversation that I had with my dad the day he informed me of the pending divorce between him and my mom. Divorce is rarely void of contention, and our family went through some difficult days. My relationship with my parents was damaged for a while as we tried to navigate through rearranged relationships and different ways of relating to one another.

I am so pleased that I can report that both of my parents experienced a resurgence in their faith in their later years. To my delight my parents actually reconciled after about three years and were actually remarried on a Sunday in the winter about the time my second daughter was born. That was a great day. The following Sunday, one week after they reconciled and remarried, my dad passed away of a heart attack. Who knows how it would have worked had he lived longer. But this I know; my mom and my dad are at peace, as am I, that they did all they could to be true to their vows when all was said and done. We are all imperfect creatures, prone to failure, but God is gracious to us in spite of our flaws. You learn from life looking back. You live your life looking forward. Do you believe that God desires what is best for you and your children? I do.

QUESTIONS FOR DISCUSSION

1. In what ways did the marriage and/or divorce of your parents affect the development of your faith?
2. What would you add to the exhortations for parents who have experienced or who are contemplating divorce?
3. In what ways does your church encourage healthy marriages? How can this be improved?
4. In what ways does your church help heal wounds that may be caused by broken marriages? How can this be improved?

CHAPTER THIRTEEN

LET'S SIT TOGETHER (IN BIG CHURCH)

Steve Parr

"One of my great regrets is that we did not sit as a family in church more often." Those words came from a father of three who attended church every week for almost thirty years as his children were growing up. He made this remark to his wife in a time of reflection shortly after his youngest daughter moved off to college. The church where the family attended was a dynamic and growing church that was reaching the community and seeing many people come to faith in Christ.

The ministry included a high-energy children's worship experience led by a capable leader. The flow of experience each Sunday typically followed a pattern where the children were dropped off in a Bible study group at 9:30 a.m. designed and appropriate for their life stage while the parents attended an adult Bible study. The children were then escorted to a children's worship service at 11:00 a.m. throughout their elementary school years (through fifth grade) while mom and dad attended the main worship service. Once the children entered the sixth grade they made the transition to "big church," as children are prone to call it if they go to a children's worship service. Once the children began to attend the adult worship service they were entering the stage of adolescence when a growing affection for peers naturally emerges and a degree of disconnect from parents increases as they seek to grow in independence. While the children in their teen years attended the same worship service as the parents, and while they would sit together occasionally, the teens would typically sit with their friends.

Reflecting on his parenting and church experience, though the family attended a very vibrant church, the father recognized with some regret that though the family went to church, and though they went to church together, they had rarely attended "together." The father had a deep conviction about the importance and value of serving the Lord in a local church and raising his family in church. However, his reflection upon the youngest daughter moving off to college highlighted a void in his heart that had not been noticed as the family made their journey together through the years. The story and the emotions are easy for me to write about because the father that I am referring to is me.

I love the church where my children grew up and I happen to still be a member of that congregation. I actually served on the church staff there for fourteen years, led the children's worship during my first year on staff, and have a high regard for the pastor and staff, including those who led the children's worship service. However, what I experienced in my heart and what I said to my wife made for an interesting comparison once this research was conducted about a year after I made the statement about my regret of not sitting in church with my family more often as our children were growing up.

What I learned through the research was quite frankly a surprise to me, although I have shared it with some who already had an inclination of what was discovered, though they had never seen it quantified. Please do not disregard or feel any disrespect no matter what side of the issue you fall on as we delve into this subject. Read on with an open mind, and prayerfully consider if any adjustments need to be made in your ministry or your family.

The research revealed that it can potentially be detrimental to separate families during the worship experience. Young adults who attended worship services that separated them from their parents when they were children were 38% more likely to have strayed as a young adult than those who were not in separate services. The statistic does not speak to the motives of church leaders who endorse or provide children's worship experiences but rather a substantial result that needs significant consideration. For those who stayed in church, they attended worship services that did not separate them from their parents when they were growing up.

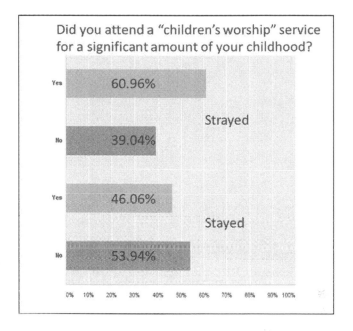

The young adults in the survey typically participated in a small group experience such as Sunday School that was designed for their life stage as preschoolers, children, and students. However, the variation related specifically to the worship experience. While the results reinforce the value of families worshipping together it is still true that you can accomplish things on an educational development level by providing designed times for age groups.

Schools do not ordinarily place second grade students with eleventh grade students or college students with fifth graders. Why not? Those who are in life stages between birth and the college years have unique needs and common intellectual capacities that can be best addressed and taken advantage of when they are grouped together. A thirty-five-year-old and a sixty-five-year-old can be placed together in a teaching environment where both can assimilate information though the age span is thirty years. However, if you place a sixteen-year-old girl in a group with a four-year-old boy, the needs and intellectual capacities are so widely varied, you will not be able to provide each with appropriate levels of instruction even though the span of difference is only twelve years. The same argument could be made to some degree for the thirty-five and sixty-five-year-old adults. Though the intellectual dynamics may not vary, the needs of each life stage often do. Small group experiences afford a church the opportunity to address specific (spiritual and intellectual) developmental needs based on the life stage of each individual.

While discipleship has an intellectual component, leaders cannot neglect the spiritual and emotional aspects that play a great, if not a greater, role in the development of one's faith. Each of these three components integrates into both the small group and worship experience as well as with one's personal spiritual experiences. How does a church maximize the spiritual, emotional, and intellectual dynamics to effectively make disciples from the youngest to the oldest? The children's worship experience has been a sincere effort to accomplish that task. I had never heard of "children's worship" when I was growing up. In the context of Christianity, while age-targeted education like Sunday School and small group Bible studies have been around for over 200 years, the children's worship is a fairly new phenomenon. Can the current erosion of attendance by young adults be connected to this? The issues are likely much broader, but we cannot ignore the facts at hand.

The children's worship experience can take several forms and does not necessarily have to separate families for three hours like it did for mine as my children grew up. You can broadly divide the types of experiences as follows:

1. The children attend the same worship service as the parents with the exception of the babies and toddlers who are tended to in a nursery or preschool environment.
2. The children attend the same worship service as the parents and a brief portion of the service includes a "children's sermon" where the kids come to the front for five minutes or so.
3. The children attend the same worship service as the parents where they worship together and then are dismissed just

before the sermon to a children's worship service for a portion of the service.

4. The children attend a separate children's worship service while the teens and adults attend the "main" worship service (or "big church" as the children sometimes refer to it).

You will also find variations on each of these four approaches and I am speaking broadly at this point. In addition, the children's worship service can vary in its implementation. Some churches with greater resources provide a very high-energy, quality experience that would equate with a spiritual version of a Nickelodeon style performance.

On the other side, I have attended churches where the children's worship experience was little more than play time and child care with little or no spiritual emphasis. You can hardly fault church leaders for wanting to provide an inviting environment for children in an effort to attract the unchurched, disciple the children of the members effectively, or provide family-friendly logistics on larger church campuses. However, the implications cannot be ignored, especially if the consequences are that the method results in fewer of the participants assimilating and staying committed to the church into their adult lives.

Could the consequences of separating children from parents during the entire worship experience be a result of the law of diminishing returns? Let me explain. What is the result if you place a child for several years (which is most of their life if they are under eleven years of age) in a high-energy, though well-meaning, children's worship service and then transition them to the adult worship service as an adolescent. To be blunt, in their mind you have moved them from an interesting experience to a very boring experience.

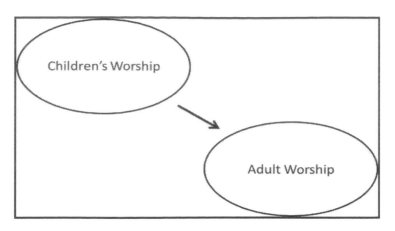

On the other hand, what if you place a child in the worship service with the parents? When he or she is nine or ten years of age, they are daydreaming, doodling, or maybe even sleeping. Suddenly, in early adolescence or just before, the pastor says something that captures their attention. I was speaking recently with a gentleman who told me how an eleven-year-old girl came up to him after church last week with excitement talking about how good the sermon was and how she had taken several pages of notes. That happened to me around twelve years of age. Somehow the lights came on and I began to understand and appreciate the message that was being preached. While I was bored as a child, my experience looked more like the image below:

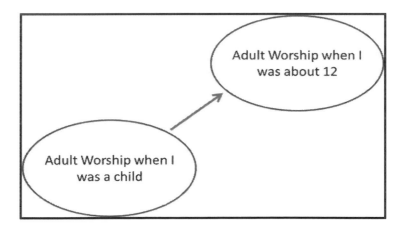

The worship experience for me was a progression instead of a digression. Could it be that this is what is happening to children who attend a charged-up children's worship? Don't misunderstand me at this point. I love children's pastors, children's ministry, churches who love children, volunteer children's workers, and children. As a matter of fact, the study found children's ministry to be important. The research revealed that a person who remembered their church as having "provided a sufficient amount of children's activities" was more likely to have stayed in church as an adult than someone whose church did not. The point here is not a negative reflection on children's ministry or children's leaders. The specific issue to grapple with based on the findings of this study is how to best approach the worship experience for your children.

While in previous chapters I have opted to share "a word for parents" and "word for pastors," I am going to combine the summary for this subject. I don't know the specific answer to this issue because it will likely vary somewhat for each family and each church. However, I do know the questions that need to be addressed.

1. *As a parent: whatever the approach to worship for my church, how can I spend more time in worship together with my children, especially when they are between the ages of six and sixteen?*

2. *As a church: how can we best balance our ministry to those who are not adults so that we can tend to the unique needs based on their life stage and still bring them together with adults to build emotional and spiritual bonds that will last for a lifetime?*

3. *As a church: can we integrate children at some (many) points into the primary worship experience?*

I do not know what you will conclude from this information or what your opinion might be prior to or after reading this. But, **if it were up to me**, here is what I would do:

1. Provide an age-graded small group experience each week to get on the level of each individual's life stage to help them grow spiritually, teach them in a way appropriate for their life

stage, encourage relationships, and help them to reach out to their peers to share the gospel. I would encourage every member to attend each week but would concede that even if they do not, when they *do* show up, they will be embraced and blessed by the experience. In addition, when they are absent, they will be prayed for, regularly contacted, and encouraged in their faith no matter the frequency of attendance patterns.

2. Provide a preschool ministry experience that is of the best quality possible based on the church's resources. Note to grandmothers: you do no one any favors by bringing your infant grandchild into the worship service. Whether he or she is cute (and I know they are adorable) or whether they are crying, they are a distraction. The expectation of a seven-year-old and a two-year-old is totally different. Somewhere around five or six years of age you can expect a child to be quiet and not to be a distraction to others even if they cannot get into every element of the worship service.

    The preschool ministry will not be simply a babysitting service. Our leaders will be trained to provide an educational/worship experience appropriate for boys and girls from birth through kindergarten age. Parents will feel good that the environment is clean, safe, and enjoyable for their child. These preschool services will be available to parents during both the small group and worship hour for babies, toddlers, and preschoolers. With that being said, I would prefer any child of any age to be at church in the service than to be at home missing the introduction to the church and development of their faith.

3. Children who are first grade and above will be invited and welcomed into the main worship service for at least half, if not all, of the service. They will sing alongside the adults, participate in the prayers, watch as friends and family members are baptized, observe mom and dad worshipping God with great joy, and be invited to participate however possible up until the sermon.

4. The sermon is a critical component of the worship service and I would be open to a couple of options. I would prefer to have an option for preschool children where they can be cared for and actually have age-appropriate worship experience

if they are not developed enough to attend without being a major disruption. The key here is the word "major." I do not think the church should allow anyone to be a "major" distraction no matter what the age, so this point is not intended as an insult to toddlers. I do not mind that a child be dealt with sometimes by a parent, but allowing a child to scream, squirm, run around, or cry for ten, fifteen, or twenty minutes is counterproductive. The pastor might as well not preach because few will be able to focus on the message. Should the church decide to dismiss those in first through third grade (or maybe even fifth) just prior to the sermon to go to a children's worship experience, I am somewhat comfortable in that they have had an opportunity to spend time in worship with their family and to begin integration into the main worship service. The transition should be much easier when they do move into the service all of the time. If this is done, I want the pastor to make "a big fuss" over them before they leave by acknowledging them or praying briefly over them before they depart. Other chapters in this book speak to the importance of this point. However, I prefer that once the child is about eight to ten, if they can attend the worship service without being a major distraction, we should invite them to attend the entire service. They may not understand everything, and may not seem to pay attention, but I am praying that "the lights will come on" and God will begin to speak into their hearts.

5. The pastor will sincerely seek to connect the sermon on some level to every life stage represented by the congregation. Yes, the sermon will generally be on an adult level and that is a majority of the audience present. However, he can acknowledge the teens, speak directly to them, encourage them, and present his message with passion, stories, and illustrations that connect with the young as well as the elder. If children are in the service, and I would prefer they would be, I want them to have a simple fill-in-the-blank outline and encourage them to take notes of the two or three key points. I have done this with effectiveness in the places I have pastored and you will be surprised that children in the third

grade will listen more than you think possible. You may call them the "pastor's pals" or something similar and consider providing incentives for those boys and girls who take notes and turn them in each week.

You obviously need to decide these issues for yourself. My youngest daughter is now a sophomore in college. She was home for about five Sundays during Christmas break. She may not have thought much about it, but each week I made a point of attending and sitting in church with her. I am thankful that she is a committed believer and seems to be on the right track spiritually for which I am most proud as a parent. She happened to attend our home church, but between me and you, I would have deferred or gone wherever she preferred for those few weeks. Thankfully, in my family, though my children attended a children's worship service that kept us separated on Sunday mornings, two of my three children are still in church as young adults. You may recall that these principles are probabilities and for each there are exceptions. But there is hardly a more beautiful picture that I could paint than that of a family all sitting together worshiping God side by side on a Sunday morning. Be sure to paint your own picture this weekend.

QUESTIONS FOR DISCUSSION

1. As a parent: whatever the approach to worship for my church, how can I spend more time in worship together with my children, especially when they are between the ages of six and sixteen?
2. As a church: how can we best balance our ministry to those who are not adults so that we can tend to the unique needs based on their life stage and still bring them together with adults to build emotional and spiritual bonds that will last for a lifetime?
3. As a church: can we integrate children at some (many) points into the primary worship experience?

CHAPTER FOURTEEN

LET THE CHILDREN COME UNTO ME

Steve Parr

Which three of the following six scenarios do you think would have the greatest impact on whether someone who grew up in church was still attending when they turned thirty?

    a. The pastor was often in their home for informal fellowship.

    b. The pastor took pride in calling down teens for talking during his sermons.

    c. The pastor attended camps alongside the staff, volunteers, children, and youth when they were provided.

    d. The pastor, though he preached well, was introverted and rarely interacted personally with children or students apart from his weekly greeting as people exited on Sunday.

    e. The pastor actively participated in Vacation Bible School.

    f. The pastor never set foot in the nursery or preschool area.

Did you like your pastor when you were growing up? Why or why not? Watching a child enthusiastically run up to his or her pastor and hug his leg is a beautiful picture. The research revealed that it actually made a significant difference if the pastor was liked by children and teens. A young adult who grew up attending church and disliked his or her pastor is 90% more likely to have strayed from church. Another way to look at this is that a person who did not like his or her pastor when young is almost twice as likely to no longer be attending, as an adult, than the person who liked his pastor when he was young. Although staff members, Bible study leaders, and volunteers play a significant role in the discipleship of children and students, the role of the pastor carries a significant weight in regard to influence. The scenarios that most likely characterize the pastor of a young adult that stayed in church would be *a, c,* and *e.*

The concept of the *priesthood of the believer* affirms that every follower of Jesus Christ has direct access to God and no individual need go through any human agent, pastor, or priest to pray, seek God's forgiveness, or to hear God speak. However, pastors and priests, by whatever title given by a particular congregation or denomination, do represent God through preaching, ministering, and leading the congregants on their journey of faith. The inability of a child to think abstractly may elevate the influence that a pastor has on a child's or teen's concept of God. Could it be that the concrete thinking of a child subconsciously links the way they perceive God to the relationship they have with God's representative when they are young? In plain language, the research revealed that a person who did not like his pastor while growing up is more inclined to dislike God and church when they become an adult and vice versa.

Do you recall this story in the Scripture?

> *Then children were brought to Him (Jesus) so He might put His hands on them and pray. But the disciples rebuked them. Then Jesus said, 'Leave the children alone, and don't try to keep them from coming to Me, because the kingdom of heaven is made up of people like this.' After putting His hands on them, He went on from there.*
> (Matthew 19:13-15 HCSB)

Jesus embraced children although the disciples somehow thought that boys and girls might be somewhat of a bother to the Lord. Jesus, as creator, certainly knew the impression that adults can have on a child and deliberately engaged with children though

His staff appeared to have thought it beneath his dignity. You see other examples of Jesus interacting with children as he receives the loaves and fish of a young boy to feed the 5,000. He raises a child from the dead. He speaks of the dire consequences for one who would harm a child when he preached the Sermon on the Mount. Jesus exemplified love for children during his earthly ministry.

Pastors need to follow the example of Jesus with understanding that their relationship, in particular, with children and teens is making an imprint and could influence whether they are still connected with the local church as an adult. A variety of leadership philosophies abound in the approach a pastor takes with his congregation. Some pastors take elevated roles where they keep a boundary between themselves and their relationship with the members. They can be mildly aloof to almost unapproachable, depending on personality and philosophy of leadership. A pastor can administrate, preach, instruct, counsel, and perform spiritual ceremonies without complaint from the church members, and still have respect and meaningful influence on a congregation and community. However, the distant approach can have detrimental consequences for the children and teens in the congregation.

May I take a moment as a fellow pastor to speak with my peers at this point? Be likeable! Is that not more of an issue of personality and temperament, you might ask? Those issues will certainly affect how natural it may or may not be to be personable. But one thing that every pastor must do in order to be an effective leader is to grow. Evaluate yourself. You may need to grow in this regard and you can. I have found that walking among the congregation for the fifteen minutes preceding the service, and dropping by three or four Bible study classes on Sunday morning to personally interact with members, pays huge dividends in the way they perceive me and my friendliness. I have the privilege of serving as an interim pastor in addition to my primary ministry responsibilities, and I have discovered that even with limited time I can connect personally with the members by simply taking moments to directly interact with as many individuals as possible. By the way, standing at the back door to greet members as they exit does not count! That is expected and you are not approaching anyone to express interest in them personally. You need to interact with the members on a personal level, and more specifically, you need to be intentional in developing relationships with the children and teens attending your local church. You do want them to like you.

You can begin by thinking of your childhood experience. What would make you like or dislike your pastor if you were a child or a teen? I am sure that you do marital counseling and perhaps you have shared how love is spelled T-I-M-E. You cannot love someone without giving, and sometimes sacrificing, time. Begin to think of how you can give time to children and students. Keith Etheridge, pastor of Double Branches Baptist Church in Lincolnton, Georgia, makes quite a sacrifice. He leads the Bible study for sixth, seventh, and eighth grade students each week the hour prior to the worship service. No one would begrudge him for taking that hour to reflect and pray in his office prior to his weekly sermon. He is making a sacrifice and the idea is somewhat genius. Think of the way this keeps him connected, not only to these middle school students, but also to those students in high school that he spent time developing the relationship with during their adolescence. Remember also, that a year is an eternity to a teen while it seems to wisp by to us as adults. At age twelve, they will have spent ten percent of their perceived life in Bible study and relationship building with their pastor. Keith can also be found on the basketball court shooting hoops and is visible at local sports and recreation activities with families. Do you think the children and teens might be inclined to like a pastor like this?

You do not have to do exactly what Pastor Etheridge is doing, but you must use your unique experiences and preferences to find a way to connect with children and teens. Does your church provide any type of summer programming for children like Vacation Bible School? I find it amazing that some pastors actually leave town on vacation during this critical week. As a pastor, you need to be right in the middle of an activity like this. Larry Wynn pastored Hebron Baptist Church in Dacula, Georgia for over thirty years, and though the congregation averaged in the thousands, he ingratiated himself with children and students by attending every church summer camp that involved children or teens. You would find him not only leading Bible study, but more importantly "hanging out" with the children and students during these experiences. His relationship with younger people was fast forwarded because so many hours of interaction were compacted into each of those critical weeks.

The pastor of a larger congregation certainly has a greater challenge in accomplishing the aim of building relationships with children and students. If you add the logistics of a children's worship experience, where they are rarely in the presence of the pastor, then the hurdle becomes even greater. That pastor must be somewhat creative, but more importantly intentional, in engaging personally with elementary school age children. The bottom line is to find opportunities to go where they are. Do not stand in a corner and observe. Get into the middle of what they are doing. Put gum in your pocket. Put a dish of candy on your desk. Let the children come to you, and do not forbid them!

Parents can take initiative on this point also. You should do anything and everything possible to make a positive connection between your pastor and your children. Begin by developing a relationship with your pastor yourself. At this point, I am not speaking of a relationship as a pastor and parishioner, but as friends. The ability to do this will vary based on the size of the congregation and the personality or leadership style of the pastor. However, if my child's spiritual health is at stake, and it is, I am not going to sit by and just hope that it happens. Find out what your family and your pastor's family have in common and connect at that point if and when possible. If you struggle on this point, then I have a solution. Everyone likes food! Initiate a meal with your pastor and his family at least once or twice each year and encourage a personal connection with your children.

Whether or not you are close to your pastor on a personal level you should also be aware of a common mistake that some parents make that could be subtly causing sabotage of their child's faith. Have you ever known a pastor who made a mistake? Are you kidding me? Pastors are human and therefore make mistakes all of the time. You may take some pride in critiquing your pastor and perhaps you know how he should be carrying out his responsibilities. But, be cautious with your comments in front of your children. The research showed that the connection between a child and his or her relationship with the pastor was substantial in their view of God and the church later in life. Therefore, be careful not to undermine that connection by verbally assaulting your pastor in front of your children. Don't get me wrong. I am not suggesting that church leaders and pastors should not confront issues that arise in terms of leadership or church life. But be wise and do what you can to ensure that your children like their pastor.

What if you are doing your best and your child still does not like the pastor? I have raised three girls and I always sought to do whatever possible to nurture their spiritual development. One of my daughters struggled in her spiritual journey as a teen, and though I was on staff and committed to my local congregation, I actually gave her liberty in terms of where she attended church as a teen. She did not have an option about attending worship any more than I gave an option about whether to attend school, whether to be in by curfew, or whether to use deodorant. You do some things because they are proper and healthy both physically and spiritually. I am going to lead my child spiritually, but as he or she goes into adolescence, I am going to defer somewhat to him or her to find an environment that will best keep them spiritually connected. If my teen does not like the pastor, I will likely be seeking another like-minded church that shares my convictions. Assuming I like my church, I can return once my teen matures and moves on. I want to do all in my power to keep my children spiritually connected, and liking the pastor is a piece of the puzzle.

Church leaders also have a role to play on this point. It begins with the pastoral interview and the scrutiny of a prospective pastor. Find out in advance about his history, philosophy, and approach to leadership style, including his relationship to children and teens. You should also be cognizant of responsibility on the back-end of the relationship. Churches do fire pastors. The research revealed to a lesser extent that having multiple pastors growing up was mildly detrimental. Having a strong relationship with a pastor is somewhat challenging if the nameplate on the office door is being changed every two years. Be good to your pastor, treat him well, and seek to keep him for a long time. He will make mistakes. Some mistakes, like moral failure, leave church leaders no choice other than to release the pastor.

Watch the way in which your church handles the circumstance where you may have to fire a pastor. Does your church have formal business meetings? If so, be sure the tone is Christ honoring when addressing difficult issues. Placing children and teens in a contentious business meeting, particularly one that is chewing up the pastor's leadership, is hazardous to the spiritual health of younger members. Do what you must, but proceed slowly, deliberately, and with Christ-like leadership. If possible, seek to coach a struggling pastor instead of running him down or running him off. In addition, remember that if a pastor must be released, in most cases he has a wife and children. Be as graceful as possible. You may take some pleasure in punishing the pastor for his mistakes but you must also consider what effect your actions will have on his innocent wife and children. A "bad church experience" was the number one self-described reason for why those who grew up in church stated that they had strayed. Do all in your power as a pastor, parent, or church leader to give children and teens a healthy church experience that helps them to connect as a disciple and servant in the local church for a lifetime.

QUESTIONS FOR DISCUSSION

1. What is it that makes a pastor "likeable" to children? To teens?
2. How might a church compensate to allow the pastor to have more interaction with the children in a circumstance where children are not included in the primary worship service?
3. How should parents respond when their teen does not like the pastor?
4. What are three ways a church can help their pastor connect better with children and teens?

CHAPTER FIFTEEN

MY YOUTH PASTOR ROCKS

Steve Parr

I did not have a youth pastor when I was growing up. I did have some good Bible study leaders. Unfortunately, I also had some poor leaders who possessed the gift of boring students with their style of teaching. However, when I was fourteen years of age, about a year or so after I came into a faith relationship with Jesus, a young adult stepped up and began pouring his life into the small group of students in our church. I felt as if he gave me special attention, and whether that was my perception or reality I cannot tell you to this day. I grew so much spiritually in those two years and recall at about age sixteen being asked to share my testimony before a large crowd at a youth crusade in our area held at the local football field. As a youth, I certainly had my struggles and my recollection is that I was very immature. But his investment in my life propelled me off of the launching pad of my spiritual journey and is a key ingredient in my continued growth as an adult.

The journey of my faith ultimately resulted in a call to preach and to serve Jesus Christ as a minister some nine years or so after a volunteer youth leader's investment. My first ten years of ministry were spent as a pastor of students at two churches. I spent an additional three years as a pastor to college age young adults. A component of my strategic thinking was to provide students with what I wanted to recieve when I was in my teen years. I focused my ministry on reaching the unchurched, sharing the gospel, teaching God's Word to students, building relationships, equipping adults to minister to students, and providing a fun and safe environment to attract students and families. I learned a lot, failed a lot, and was blessed by God to see hundreds of students come to faith in Jesus. Both groups that I led grew and by God's grace made an impact on many lives. Although my ministry focus has changed in these later years, I still enjoy those occasional opportunities when I am invited to speak and minister to teens and college students.

The research on young adults who grew up in church revealed several key points about ministry to students. For example, recalling their church as having provided sufficient "youth activities" when they were growing up had a positive correlation to those who stayed in church as young adults. Those going through their adolescent years have unique needs and challenges that need to be addressed by the local church. A young adult who attended a church with a ministry to students was more likely to have stayed as an adult, and one who attended a church without a ministry to students was more likely to have strayed. That is a simple starting point for a church and a critical concern for a parent.

A church does not have to employ a youth pastor in order to have a significant youth ministry. That is good news. The young adult who led the ministry for students when I was growing up was a volunteer and he made a big difference. The leadership of the ministry to students must begin with the pastor, and I will refer you to the previous chapter to be reminded of the value and importance of his relationship with the teens in the church. A full-time vocational youth minister can be greatly advantageous because of the expertise, time investment, and leadership of volunteers that he or she can provide.

However, the research revealed another important point that fits well here. Having a youth ministry was important, but the respondents revealed no connection between having had a youth pastor on the church staff during one's teen years and whether or not that person was active in church as an adult. A deeper look at this point will reveal that it is actually positive rather than negative. Fewer than one-fourth of churches employ a vocational youth pastor. The encouraging news here is that your church does not have to have a paid youth pastor in order for the faith of your children to thrive.

It is not a poor reflection on the role of a youth pastor as much as a correlation to the size of churches. Congregations that have the resources to employ staff members who can give attention to the faith development of students are blessed and should take advantage of the opportunity. In the absence of those resources, volunteers who are willing to invest spiritually into the lives of middle school and high school students can equally make a great impact. Having a staff youth minister is good, but having a ministry focused on students is essential. Find a way, no matter what size church you attend, to minister to youth.

Let us now move on to the value of having a youth pastor on the church staff, not as a volunteer, but part-time or full-time employed by the church. The research revealed that those who had the leadership of a vocational youth minister were 16% more likely to still be in church if they liked him or her when growing up. A variety of qualities are desired in a vocational youth leader. A church should certainly seek someone with strong moral character, spiritual depth, Bible knowledge, teaching ability, leadership skills, administrative gifts, and creativity just to name a few, and this list is not intended to be exhaustive. Do not neglect, however, to place a high premium on people skills. We all know people who:

- Teach well but cannot relate well to individuals one on one.
- Organize well but work mostly from a desk.
- Innovate and create but cannot resolve conflicts.
- Have Bible knowledge and possess a harsh spirit.
- Have strong moral character but lean toward introversion.
- Have charisma with teens and cannot relate to adults.

No candidate for your youth pastor position will have a perfect blend of skills, but one's moral character must not be neglected and you should not minimize the value of people skills. These skills can be developed but at the least the roots should be very evident. The ability of a leader to endear himself or herself to people builds trust, makes people feel valued, reduces conflict, opens ears to his or her teaching, and maximizes influence which the research proves to be long-lasting.

The research further highlighted the value of consistency and longevity. A mildly negative correlation was noted between those who had strayed from church and those who had several different youth pastors when they were growing up. I recently spoke with someone who reflected this very point. The church has gone through four youth ministers in the past five years and the high school juniors and seniors have no enthusiasm whatsoever for the newest leader. They feel they are constantly being abandoned and unfortunately they are very likely to stray from church as young adults. Rotating youth pastors in and out every couple of years is worse for the students than having no youth pastor at all. For the prospective youth minister, do not even consider the position if you are not committed to four to five years or more. For the church: seek to stay with a youth pastor long-term; and if he or she makes mistakes you should try to coach them if possible instead of moving them along. I know that circumstances are more complex than those last two statements, but you should be prayerful and take this research into consideration when making these types of decisions.

Here is a review to this point of what the research revealed about youth ministry and its correlation with those who stay.

1. Having a strategic youth ministry in any size church positively correlates with those who grow up in church staying when they are adults.
2. While calling a part-time or full-time youth pastor to minister to students has many advantages, there is no correlation between whether a young adult was led by a volunteer or vocational leader and whether they were in church as a young adult. The key is that they did have adults from the church investing in them during their teen years.
3. For those who had a vocational youth pastor, they are much more likely to stay in church if they like him or her.
4. Those who had multiple vocational youth pastors when growing up were somewhat more likely to have strayed.

A Word for Pastors

Remember that the ministry to students begins with you. The youth leaders, whether volunteer or vocational, supplement what you do. They cannot do what they need to do without your leadership, affirmation, support, and partnership. Please be sure you read chapter fourteen and understand how critical your role is in the lives of teens and children growing up in your church. You can delegate the ministry to others but only to a degree. You will not be able to disconnect yourself, and the research shows that you may be undermining the faith of young people if and when you do. I recently visited Parker Memorial Church in Anniston, Alabama where I found another pastor teaching Sunday morning Bible study for fifth and sixth graders. That is a sacrifice, and it is also genius. At that point in time, those two years represent almost ten percent of the lives those ten and eleven-year-old students, and they are connecting to the pastor in a powerful way.

Second, insist that your congregation develop and continually improve on a ministry targeted to the needs of teens. George Barna indicates that nearly half of all Americans who accept Jesus Christ as their Savior do so before reaching the age of thirteen (43%), and that two out of three born again Christians (64%) made that commitment to Christ before their eighteenth birthday.[29] These are crucial years for evangelism and discipleship affecting the health and potential growth of your congregation, as well as the key to sustaining the strength of the faith of those who grow up in your congregation.

You have responsibilities and obligations that make it challenging to give your time to the students. You need not give all of your time, but you must give some of your time. You will need help. Therefore, third, enlist a team and meet with them regularly to evaluate, plan, and implement a ministry of discipleship and evangelism for students. Perhaps your church has the resources to employ a vocational youth pastor. That is great and you should take advantage of it. He or she will be able to carry a much greater responsibility for the leadership and equipping of the volunteers. But, do not disconnect. Work as a mentor and partner while seeking ways to maintain connections personally with the students. You may not lead the weekly Bible study, but you will do well to attend their camps, go to a variety of community activities throughout the year that involve your students, acknowledge them during your preaching, and personally engage with them as you go about your work day by day. Be the initiator. Be a partner. Be known as a "youth ministry friendly pastor."

A Word for Parents

My intent in the following word of advice is not an endorsement of the current wave of church consumerism and church hopping that has become prevalent. However, the spiritual development and needs of your children trump my concerns with those issues. The adolescent years are critical, and as a parent you should do all within your power to provide the healthiest church environment you can for your teen. You will likely struggle on some levels even when the environment for your teen is great. Begin with the church where you currently attend. As you read this book you will discover actions that you can take that can make a difference in the likelihood that your child will be faithfully serving Jesus into their adult years. I am not suggesting that you create a fuss, but I am exhorting you to provide leadership where needed. Begin where you are and work with your church leaders to provide the best possible environment for your children and other teens.

Should you get resistance, fail to get cooperation, or discover that your church is not committed to providing a nurturing environment for teens, then prayerfully consider what is best for your child. In some cases, you may need to leave for a season, attend a church where your child's spiritual needs can be best met, and then return once they have moved on. The issue is not about money, although anyone can appreciate that greater resources are advantageous. A healthy ministry to students is built on people. If a church has people, and in my experience most of them do, then a ministry for students can be developed and provided. It comes down to priorities more than it does to dollars.

Your child needs other spiritual voices singing God's tune to them when they go through adolescence. A child's quest for independence is a healthy though tumultuous aspect of a parent-child relationship. Your child will listen to you less and less and may not listen at all at some points during the teen years. As the parent of three grown children I want to encourage you at this point. They will usually come full circle and begin seeking your wisdom again as they transition from adolescence to adulthood. For those parents who do not go to church, who is speaking into the lives of their teens on a spiritual level during these critical years? More than likely it is no one and they will not likely be found in church as adults.

You need someone to continually emphasize the same messages that you would to your teens if they would listen. You need the reinforcement even if you have the compliant child who appears to be listening to you. Do all that you can to connect your children to other adults as well as other teens who have deeply rooted faith and strong moral character. You need to connect your teens to environments where multiple layers of opportunities and relationships exist. Here is why: if they do not like one particular youth leader or youth pastor, but they have two or three other adults they are bonded with, you can help them overcome that relationship issue.

No one likes everyone, and no one is liked by everyone. The issue is not always spiritual in nature. Different personalities relate differently to other types of personalities. Just because your teen does not like a particular adult leader does not mean that adult does not love the Lord. Place your teen in an environment where there are a few if not many adults who work with teens, not just an individual leader. In summary, plug your children into environments where people are saying to them the same things you are saying. In this way the message is delivered even if and when they do not hear it from you.

A Word for Youth Pastors

You would not recognize me as a youth pastor if we met because I have a few more miles on me now. I think it is harder to be a minister to students now than it was when I served in that role. However, some things never change. The dilemma that you face is that while you should not be a "people pleaser" or do things for the sake of being "liked," you must be "liked" in order to have the attention and devotion of those who are your followers. I want to recommend a classic book that I read many years ago that can give you guidance and instruction without compromising that delicate balance. Download or pick up a copy of Dale Carnegie's *How to Win Friends and Influence People.* You will receive practical wisdom for progressing in your people skills that will serve you well in any role.

While you obviously understand the importance of theological training, character that is above reproach, sensitivity to security issues related to working with adolescents, how to teach God's

Word on their level, and how to create an environment that engages students, I want to challenge you to also focus on developing these skills that will serve you well as a youth pastor:

1. How to impact students who may not like you (even when you've done nothing to offend them).
2. How to minister to the core members of your group.
3. How to minister to students who are not in the core of your group.
4. How to enlist and equip adult leaders to serve alongside.
5. How to move students from membership to leadership.

The book you are reading is not about youth ministry, but it contains huge implications for your ministry. As you lead your students to grow, do not neglect your growth. I teach that the leadership of spiritual leaders rides on two rails and the principles hold true for you also. Give attention without fail to your own personal spiritual growth. That is the top priority for your leadership and will fuel your effectiveness. However, place a premium on your skills growth as well or you will find yourself close to God in front of a very limited human audience. You forfeit your ability to lead at the point you fail to grow. These two rails are essential if you are to give students what they need to develop a faith relationship that will continue into their adult years.

There is one more thing I want to add. If no one has told you lately, thanks for what you do! Serving students and investing in their lives makes a difference in your church, your community, and the churches of the future. Ministry to students yields fruit that you will be able to observe for all of your life. Keep investing so that others will be prepared to take the gospel to the next generation and beyond!

QUESTIONS FOR DISCUSSION

1. What are the strengths of the ministry to teens in your church?
2. How can your church improve the ministry to teens in your church?
3. How are volunteer youth leaders utilized in your church? How are they equipped? How can this be improved?
4. What makes a teen "like" his or her youth pastor?
5. What role does longevity play in the relationship between teens and youth leaders?

CHAPTER SIXTEEN

MY PARENTS ARE "ALL IN"

Tom Crites

"Raise your hand if you can say that your mom dragged you to church every time the doors were open..." I had no reason to trust the person asking this question, other than the fact that he was my professor and I was his student, so I wrestled with allowing him a sneak peek into my personal life. I had noticed that he was a smoker (in the days before smoking was banned on campuses) and a curser (in the days when curse words were not everyday vernacular). Perhaps I was intimidated or shocked, but I slowly and cautiously raised my hand through the smoky silence, unsure as to why my philosophy professor was interested in knowing my church-going habits. Boy, was I ever sorry for that action. His thickly browed eyes honed in on me like a laser. "Uh-huh," he said. Thankfully, another student's hand slowly went up, then another. His eyes left my chair and focused in on them. A slight smirk snuck out from behind his mustache; I had made his life interesting. From that day forward, he identified me and the other unfortunate hand raisers as the "ones he intended to fix in the next thirteen weeks." He was determined to flush all the churchy malaise from our pitiful brains and fill the void with pure, unrestricted doubt.

That was a challenging semester for me. When I reflect back on that experience, I admit that I was shaken. It was really the first time in my life that my faith and tradition had been placed into question.

I came from a small coal mining and farming community where just about everyone was connected to a local church. But now, someone was assuming that because I was raised in church I was damaged and needed intellectual repair. I felt hurt, confused, and a bit ticked off. He had insulted me—and *my mother*. The professor's techniques, focused on intellectual doubt and humanism, had also challenged my personal faith experiences. After a season of spiritual wrestling, my faith was battered and bruised—but not broken. I never would have made it through that term without the support and example of my parents.

My parents loved God and loved His church. They lived out their faith at home and served the church in every way imaginable. My mother taught small group Bible studies, led girls in discipleship, sang in the choir, helped with the benevolence ministry, and probably had a key to the building. My dad was equally connected, serving as a deacon of the church, leading boys in Bible study, teaching young adults, singing in the choir... you get my point. My parents were "all in." Their commitment to the church and steady example at home demonstrated to me that their faith was real. They loved serving the Lord in His church and taught me to love it, too.

Young Adults Who Stay

Among the young adults surveyed, the ones who stayed in church had similar testimonies about their parents. Those who stayed said their father had served in various roles in the church where they grew up. The same could be said for those sharing about their mother's leadership in the church. The young adults more prone to stray were 50% more likely to say that their mother attended church but did not serve as a leader, or that she did not attend church. It was evident from my research that young adults staying in church had parents who were actively serving in a local church. There was a noticeable distinction between the parents' attendance and serving. Similarly, young adults were more likely to stay in church if their dad held a "definitive" role in the church. In other words, more of those who stayed in the church remembered their father being a deacon or a Bible teacher rather than serving in "various roles." My research demonstrated that these young adults were 16% more likely to stay if dad held a more memorable role in the church.

In Luke 2:52, Jesus is described as growing in *...wisdom and stature, and in favor with God and with people* (HCSB). This sentence summarizes Jesus' life between the ages of twelve and thirty. As brief as it is, it still describes the reasons why children must be led. Children are not born with wisdom but rather are born in weakness. They do not automatically or spontaneously have favor with men and their sin nature alienates them from God's favor. John MacArthur describes this as a "disaster."[30] To help alleviate this disaster, one must train up a child in the way he should go. Proverbs 22:6 promises that when a trained child is mature, he will not stray from this path. Children need to be taught how to have favor with God and with man. This can be accomplished effectively through commitment in the home *and* the church. Children who have effective "faith coaches," namely parents, are much more likely to continue practicing their faith than those who are left to figure it out on their own.

James Dobson wrote the following, which supports these findings: "(Children) want to know what is most important to us. If we hope to instill within them a faith that will last a lifetime, they must see and feel our passion for God."[31] From our research, the best place for a child to see his parents' passion for the Lord is in the home *and* in the church. Both must be present. Do not make the mistake of thinking that you can fake passion for God either in the home or at church. Children have an innate radar that can detect any monkey business. Any cracks in your ethics or morals will be intensified in their lives. Like it or not, your faith—or the lack thereof—makes a difference to your children. Dobson says parents can count on the faith or faithlessness demonstrated by their children to be a solid reflection of the parents' spiritual life.[32] Parents must understand the responsibility they have for the faith development of their children.

The important thing to note here is that young adults remember the roles their parents played in church, whether they participated or refrained from involvement. It made an impression on them. They remember that their parents held important leadership positions that demonstrated commitment and spiritual maturity. The people who stayed in church had parents who were "all in." And now that they are adults themselves, they are continuing not simply a tradition but a biblical mandate to exercise one's spiritual gifts to strengthen the body of Christ.

When asked why they have stayed in church, the second most common self-described reason for staying was that they are "personally serving" in a leadership position at their church. You may recall that Jesus was once asked to declare the most important of all of the commandments. Jesus knew that the Old Testament contained over 600 distinct commands. Perhaps the religious leaders of the day thought they might trip Him up by tasking Him to single out only one of hundreds of commandments as the most important. However, Jesus did not hesitate. He said to them, *"Love the Lord your God with all your heart, with all your soul, and with all your mind."* (Matthew 22:37 HCSB) Serving is evidence of obedience to this supreme command. Do not let your children see you serving or loving God with "some" of your heart or even with "most" of your heart, but with "all" of your heart. Let them see that you are "all in," and you will know that you are demonstrating that a relationship with God, though centered in the heart, is expressed through the feet and hands as we serve Him in our congregations and in the community.

A Word for Parents

Your children are watching you. I know you love your children and want the best for them, but please understand that I am not saying you should call your pastor today and volunteer for everything you can or grace the doors every time they are open. That is not going to make the desired impression. Instead, first seek to walk close to the Lord personally. Be sure you are making a priority of spending time in God's Word daily as you seek an intimate relationship with Jesus Christ. Make sure that your heart is pure and your will is in line with God's. Then, as a natural outpouring of your closer walk with God, you will desire to exercise your spiritual gifts in service to others. Your children will see the growth and the maturity.

For those of you who feel you have already blown it, begin right where you are. The most important thing for you is to renew your close relationship to the Lord. Ask Him to lead you to be a better example to your children. Consider rebuilding your relationships with your church. Perhaps certain church members have hurt you in the past. Seek reconciliation where you can. However, if you cannot, then please remember this: Do not fail to serve the Lord because of the actions or attitudes of His followers in a local congregation. Why withhold service to God because of the actions of human agents? Responding maturely to your hurts and disappointments plays a crucial role in your spiritual health, but also in the example you set for your children. Don't allow your hurts to potentially keep your children from a close walk with Jesus Christ. This is crucial to your spiritual maturity and your child's development. Apologize to your kids if you must. Be honest with them about your failures and shortcomings. Express your renewed desire to be a good model for them and then work at it with all of your heart.

If you are currently leading in a local church, you must ask yourself some questions. How am I doing? Am I exercising my spiritual gifts in service to a local congregation and my community? Would the Lord be pleased by my service? Am I doing my best to serve God in my service roles? Is my leadership a natural expression of my daily walk with God? Serving the Lord in His church has so many associated benefits. One we have noticed is the benefit of demonstrating to our children that our faith is real. A tangible way to encourage your kids to stay in church is to personally serve the Lord in His church.

A Word for Pastors

I want to encourage you as a pastor to allow your members to serve the Lord in His church. Having served in a church, I know that sometimes it is easier to just do something yourself. It takes energy and time to enlist and train people to serve and lead. And there are certain inherent risks when releasing responsibilities to volunteers. However, it is worth it. People need to serve God in His local church. They need to be stretched and challenged. They need to give back their gifts and talents as offerings to the Lord. Children need to see their parents and other adults serving the Lord and demonstrating a real faith.

What is the strategy for your church when it comes to enlistment of volunteers, discovery of spiritual gifts, and development of leaders? One common mistake is to place all enlistment in the hands of a committee that focuses on an eight- to twelve-week segment of time preceding the new calendar year or academic year. Enlistment and leadership development need to develop into a perpetual twelve months-a-year approach to get the fullest benefit. Do you offer multiple windows of time and entry points for service? Do not make every opportunity a twelve-month commitment. Allow members a variety of ministry opportunities with a broad range of time commitments—from weekend opportunities, to three-month commitments, to one-year covenants—based on the level of ministry and expectation for the various service roles. What is your plan for equipping church members to be servants for the Lord? That is a key component and a definitive part of your responsibility according to Ephesians 4:11-12. People enjoy doing what they are skilled at doing. Equipping is the means by which skills are sharpened and, in turn, ministry is enjoyed.

Ask yourself these questions as you consider developing leaders in your church. Am I effectively discipling leaders? When recruiting people to serve, am I thinking about kingdom work, or just trying to get a job done? Am I releasing people to do God's work in His church? Am I helping the current leaders in my church develop spiritually? Is my spiritual leadership a help or a hindrance to the growth of those I lead?

QUESTIONS FOR DISCUSSION

1. What is your leadership role in the church and is it clear and identifiable to your children?
2. Thinking about your leadership in the church, how are you training your child to love God and His church?
3. What is the strategy of your local congregation for enlisting and equipping leaders? What can be done to improve the process and what role might you play in making it more effective?
4. How can you help others reach their potential in serving the Lord in His church?

CHAPTER SEVENTEEN

JUST GETTING STARTED

Steve Parr

M*ilestone*: an action or event marking a significant change or stage in development. I have had a few of those along my journey—my salvation, my first day of school, my first date, engagement to my future wife, our wedding day, my ordination, the birth of our children, and our 25th wedding anniversary just to name a few. Though I have never ranked the milestones, I would have to place my high school graduation near the top. I would not place it there because of its value so much as for the degree of excitement it generated. The graduation marked a transition that brought opportunities over the following ninety days including my first full-time summer job, my move away from my parents and family to be on my own, the beginning of my college studies, new relationships, and more freedom than I had ever known. I was six months shy of my eighteenth birthday when this took place.

My spiritual journey was progressing, having placed my faith in Jesus just before my thirteenth birthday. I made mistakes and sometimes gave into temptations that are common to the teen experience, but I always experienced a deep sense of conviction and quickly responded and repented. I attended worship and Bible study every week without any prompting from my parents. My faith was genuine and early on was driven from within by the work of the Holy Spirit in my life. My college commitment was three months away and I had a summer at home to enjoy before moving away.

The Bible study that I attended regularly through high school met on Sunday mornings prior to the worship service and I was close to the five other students who attended alongside me. I transitioned through the years from children's Sunday School classes for grades one through three and then for fourth and fifth grades. From there I went to the class for sixth through eighth graders and then made the leap into the high school Sunday School class in the ninth grade. I was in the high school group for four of my seventeen years of life to that point. If you remove the first two years of which I have no memory, I had spent a quarter of my life with this group studying God's Word and growing together. My graduation marked another transition that was very important. Now that my high school journey was over, the time had come to transition to the next level of Bible study designed for those who completed high school and were about to embark on their path to college, an apprenticeship, the military, or to learn a trade.

At this point I encountered a problem that is all too typical in the local church even today. The next group beyond the "youth Sunday School class" was the "young married class." In my eyes they were not young. They were married, but at this stage of my life I was not interested in marriage and could not relate. My church simply did not have any ministry that focused on those who had graduated from high school but were not yet ready for married life. And that is a problem. I was able to overcome this barrier most likely because I moved off to college and made spiritual connections on the college campus and in a local church that had a ministry focused on college age young adults.

The research revealed a gap that has a definitive effect on the likelihood that a person who grows up in church will still be attending as an adult. First of all, 61% of those in the survey who no longer attended church strayed during their college years. Please note that I use the term "college years" to describe the stage of life between high school graduation and about twenty-two years of age and acknowledge that not everyone goes to college. However, these years are critical in the spiritual development of those who come to faith prior to eighteen years of age and the research revealed several factors that need the attention of church leaders. One of those issues relates to the way churches approach ministry to college age young adults.

One of my areas of expertise is that of equipping leaders and growing Bible study groups in the local church. Most churches provide a Sunday morning Bible study experience preceding the worship service. The groups are labeled differently in various churches but go by titles such as Sunday Morning Bible Study, Sunday School, Bible Study Fellowship, Small Groups, Connect Groups, and Life Bible Study Groups just to name a few. While a majority of churches offer these groups on Sunday mornings, some churches because of space limitations or as a strategy offer Bible study groups at other times during the week. In addition, the groups are generally organized by life stage. Preschool children are generally placed together. Children are ordinarily placed in groups based on the grade they attend in school, and students in middle school and high school are similarly organized. Adults are loosely organized by life stage from young married adults through the senior adults. The structure varies from church to church based on the size of the congregation, the facilities available, and the philosophy of each church toward Christian education and discipleship.

I have been privileged to equip and consult in several thousand congregations over the past thirty years. If I have an audience of ten pastors and ask them about the organization of their Bible study groups, which group do you think is least likely to be represented by those churches? The answer is easy and all too common. The least likely group is one that is focused on college age young adults. You can test this for yourself. Ask ten friends from different churches or ten pastors if they have Bible study groups for preschoolers, children, students (in grades seven through twelve), college age young adults, young married adults, median age adults, and senior adults. You will no doubt discover that the least represented group is for college age young adults. Is it a coincidence that the timeframe in which a former attendee is most likely to stop participating is also the stage at which churches are least likely to provide ministry and Bible study? Other factors certainly play a role in the possibility that those who grow up in church drop out during college years. Fortunately, some who drop out will reconnect. However, church leaders have a responsibility for the discipleship of all members in all life stages, and the research reveals a glaring gap.

The church that provides a ministry focused on college age young adults makes a definitive difference. The research revealed that those who grew up attending church were 33% more likely to have strayed if they remained in the same town and the church they attended did not have a ministry for college age young adults. In other words, those who attended a church that provides targeted ministry for post high school graduates were more likely to still be in church as adults. What about your church? Does your church provide ministry to continue developing the faith of those ages eighteen to twenty-two? This life stage is a great opportunity for the church. Young adults in this age range certainly have their struggles but they also possess passion, energy, influence over younger students, and freedom from schedules that will overtake them as jobs progress and families develop. In case you did not know, they will not bring your church a lot of financial resources. They may even cost you financially. However, if they are more likely to continue attending as adults, those resources will be reaped in the future. I believe you would agree that resources should not be the motivating factor anyway. The Great Commission compels believers to make disciples of "all nations." What does that mean? It means all people in all places in all life stages. College age young adults are not exempt from our responsibilities as a local church.

A friend of mine surveyed a small group of college age young adults recently and asked how they thought the church perceived them as a group. The top two responses he received:

1. They think we are all sowing our wild oats and that we have no concern for spiritual matters.
2. They are not even aware that we exist. They ignore us.

Ouch! They mirrored what the research revealed but put it in blunt terms that church leaders need to hear. The college age young adults in your community provide an opportunity that is equally rewarding for the church and for the post high school graduates as well. Understand that the responsibility for discipleship does not conclude at the high school graduation of your students; it is a time for each church to acknowledge their responsibility and opportunity for those who are not finishing their education but just getting started. Therefore, every church:

1. **Must seek to provide discipleship and Bible study opportunities for everyone in every life stage,** including college age young adults.

2. **Must understand that a college in the community is not the criteria** for whether a church has a ministry for college age young adults or not. Every community has some, if not many, young adults between the ages of eighteen and twenty-two.

3. **Must understand that ministry to college age young adults is rewarding but also one of the more challenging ministries a church can have.** The struggles common to this life stage, the wavering and development of commitment levels, the newfound freedom they are experiencing, and the additional influences that affect their thinking make up a recipe for difficult ministry. Leaders may have to work twice as hard for half of the results and they can easily become discouraged. Do not give up. Ministry to this age group makes a profound difference in the long term.

4. **Must focus more on what they have than what they do not have.** Many church leaders upon reflecting on this will be tempted to excuse themselves from this issue because they are fewer in number or lack resources. However, the two key resources needed are available to every church. The first is the power of God. The second is a willing leader. Someone must step up. It may be the pastor, a volunteer, or the parent of a college age young adult. Every church makes choices. Choose to fill this gap.

5. **Must have a conversation with young adults.** The conversation can be informal and you may not like everything you hear. However, they may be willing to step up into leadership when they know the church cares and is committed to meeting their unique spiritual needs. You need not adopt every recommendation that a group of young

adults suggests. But if you apply and implement a few of their ideas it can go a long way to appealing to them and helping them stay connected during this critical stage of their spiritual development.

A Word for Pastors

You have been presented yet another challenge and you no doubt already have a full plate. How do you proceed? First, begin with number five on the previous list. Gather a group of younger adults in your home or at a restaurant and have the conversation. You say you only have one or two in this age group? Invite them and ask them to bring a friend or two. You say you have none? Work with members to identify five or six young adults to participate with you in a focus group. Here is why. This conversation may go a long way to giving you credible resolutions to this challenge and those who participate are more likely to offer their help than those who have never been engaged in such a conversation.

You may actually have to provide some leadership initially. The root of a good ministry for this age group is a Bible study. It does not have to meet on Sunday morning. That actually gives you some flexibility. I started a Bible study for college age young adults in my home some years back. I served as the pastor to students and noted that this gap began to grow as students graduated from my ministry. I had about six students attend each Friday night, but within a couple of years the ministry began to thrive and others were enlisted to provide leadership.

Begin praying now for a leader to step up and to give attention to this age group. The weakest way to enlist is to announce a need from the pulpit. Follow the model of Jesus from Luke 6:12-16 when He enlisted the Apostles from among his disciples. You will note that He prayed all night and as God revealed to Him those He should call, He went to them directly and appealed to them to become His Apostles. If you have no one in your church, contact a pastor from a thriving church and challenge him to send someone on mission to serve your young adults for a season.

Here is what I learned to be the key to effective ministry among this age group when I served as a college pastor for three years. In regard to activities, treat them like high school students. By that I mean that you should work with them to provide lots of fellowship opportunities where they can have fun and invite friends. In regard to Bible study, treat them like adults. I heard Dr. Alvin Reid state recently, "If students can tackle trigonometry, they can tackle theology." Dig deep in Bible study, theology, and apologetics. They are asking questions and wrestling with issues and this is a wide open opportunity for you and your church. Remember, for most churches this subject is sadly not even on their radar. That opens the doors even wider for your church to minister and to make a difference in the lives of post high school graduates in your community. Get to it!

A Word for Parents

Do not wait until your child graduates to grapple with this issue. If your child is young or in the early high school years, now is the best time to determine what you might do to make a difference. Does your church have a ministry for college age young adults? If the answer is "no," are you convinced that it needs one? If that is the case and no one has stepped up, I know what the immediate resolution is. It is you! You may feel unqualified, ill-equipped, and unprepared. However, this ministry needs to be up and going before your child graduates. You have no time to waste. Perhaps you can work with your pastor to enlist someone. If not, the answer is you.

Perhaps you might counter by arguing that your child is going off to college in another town so this does not apply to your family. The issue at hand is not about your child but about all college age young adults in your community. In addition, your child will be home in the summer months and for the holiday breaks. Will ministry be provided for them when they are home or will they be expected to go to the young married adult Bible study? Here is what you will discover. It will be easier for them to skip Bible study if nothing is provided and in turn easier for them to disconnect from the church. There are no guarantees being offered. You could do all of this and your child may still stray. Hopefully that will not happen. But even if he did, you could take solace in the fact that you invested in others as others have invested in your child.

I am about to make a point and I want to be clear that I am not suggesting that you change churches. My first appeal to you is to work with church leaders to provide a ministry for this age group and to step up yourself if needed. But if your church is resistant to this age group, you may have to make a difficult decision. Your first responsibility for discipleship begins in your own home, and it is critical that you place your children in the best possible environment to ensure the maximum probability that their faith will grow, thrive, and endure. Partner with your pastor, work with your church, challenge your fellow parents, and in the end, do what you must do to help students make the post high school transition spiritually as well as educationally. Because, in reality, high school grads are just getting started.

QUESTIONS FOR DISCUSSION

1. Why do you think churches struggle with ministry to this life stage?
2. What is the next Bible study group available for students in your church once they graduate from high school? Is that group meeting the need? Why or why not?
3. Describe the ministry to college age young adults provided by your church.
4. Discuss one action that you read about in this chapter that could benefit your church and the college age young adults in your community.

CHAPTER EIGHTEEN

WHAT'S YOUR MAJOR?

Steve Parr

My grandfather sat next to my aunt at my college graduation. Many of my classmates were commended for their academic achievements. The Dean of Academic Affairs called their names and followed by pronouncing: "*Cum Laude*," or "*Summa Cum Laude*," or "*Magna Cum Laude*." My grandfather turned to my aunt and said, "There sure are a lot from that Laude family graduating today!" It was a happy day and certainly marked another important milestone in my journey.

I knew where I wanted to go to college before I completed my junior year of high school. My desire was to major in education so I could teach high school and coach baseball. I went to a small, private college located about a two-hour drive from my hometown. It was far enough away that I could not come home at night and close enough to get home for weekends when desired. When I attended Shorter College (now Shorter University), it could best be described as a school with a strong Christian environment. Although there were no standards for chapel or church attendance, and many of the students and faculty were not Christians, a significant percentage of both were strong believers.

I wavered slightly in my church attendance during the first weeks, having been displaced from the church where I grew up. I also struggled socially for the first two to three months and that was a turning point for me in and of itself. I had to learn to reach out, initiate conversation, and be friendly to strangers instead of sitting back waiting on them to approach me. My church attendance fit the same profile as I sat back waiting on someone to invite me to attend. God spoke to my heart and I was reminded that, "A man who has friends must himself be friendly." (Proverbs 18:24 NKJV) The first semester was a lonely learning experience. My faith helped me turn it around. I connected with a strong evangelistic church and began taking more initiative in relationships. By my sophomore year I was tapped for an organization that recognized eight students for their school involvement and spirit and capped my college career as President of the senior class. I struggled, grew, matured, met my future wife, made life-long friendships, and graduated. My faith grew stronger, and though I did not know it at the time, God would change my direction four years following college from teaching to preaching as I accepted His call.

In the midst of the college experience, I wrestled with theological, moral, and ethical issues. I had strong roots, but my thinking was tested by new ideas and many people who skillfully articulated opposing concepts that contradicted my own belief system. I am reminded of the illustration at the end of the *Sermon on the Mount* in the seventh chapter of Matthew where the wind blew, the rain fell, and the floods rose, but the house stood because it was built on a solid foundation. I experienced the storms of intellectual arguments, doubters, and opposing ideas, but my spiritual house withstood because I entered college with a strong faith. I believe the Christian college enhanced my growth because I never felt alone in my faith in spite of the loneliness I experienced initially which was part of God's plan to help me grow socially. College was a great experience for me on many levels, and if I could repeat it, I would still choose Shorter College.

My youngest daughter is attending college now and my oldest two are both college graduates. My eldest daughter commented upon graduating that she did not realize she had a choice about whether to attend college or not. That statement made me feel good about my parenting because I always sought to balance high expectations for my children with freedom to make choices. However, I am well aware that one need not go to college in order to excel or to lead a productive life.

Almost 70% of high school graduates will enroll in college and almost 60% of those will graduate within six years.[33] That means that about 42% of high school grads will go on to graduate from college within a few years. Anecdotal stories of individuals who opt not to attend college or those who attend and fail to graduate yet go on to start businesses, make good salaries, and become productive citizens are not difficult to find. However, the research revealed a surprising correlation between the college experience and the likelihood that someone who grows up in church stays connected as an adult.

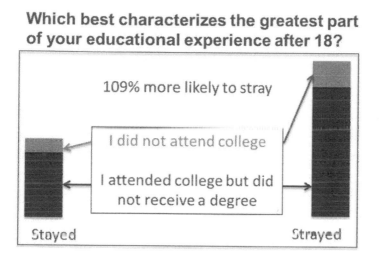

Which best characterizes the greatest part of your educational experience after 18?

In summary, the results showed that those who grew up in church and had remained faithful as adults had very likely attended college and graduated. This particular point may be unique to North American culture and you will learn what we believe to be the root of the issue later in this chapter. The results showed that a young adult was 109% more likely to have strayed from church if they did not go to college at all. That is a huge number. You would do well to read Chapter Seventeen at this point if you happened to skip over it because that chapter documents how young adults who attend a church without a ministry to college age young adults are much more inclined to stray and never return.

A similar result, though smaller, was noted if they attended college but failed to graduate. In addition, the research revealed the value of attending a Christian college over a secular institution. Young adults are 90% more likely to stay in church if they attend a college that has a strong Christian environment. The fact that a high school grad elects to attend a Christian college may be a reflection of a deep faith commitment that is further strengthened by what they will be exposed to on a Christian-oriented campus. This factor would mirror my personal journey as I experienced some initial struggles and wrestled with intellectual issues of faith. However, I was surrounded by a large majority of believers and worked through it all with a strong commitment.

Attending a Christian college for the believer who grows up in church can be equated with "home field advantage." In athletics, a team tends to perform better on their home field than they do when playing on the field of the opponent. It is true of all sports on all levels. Teams can lose at home and they can win on the road. However, when you add up all games, more teams win at home and more teams lose on the road. When you play on your home field, a majority of the crowd is cheering you on, encouraging you, working to distract your opponent, and to do all in their power to give you a winning edge. However, when you play on the road, people are booing you, shouting insults, calling you names, calling your mother names, distracting you by all means, and doing all in their power to cause you to fail. When you place a student who grew up in church in an environment where the professors are believers, the student population is largely Christian, and spiritual growth opportunities abound, you are giving them the ultimate home field advantage. That will not guarantee that they still serve Christ as adults, but the probability that they will is greatly increased.

The issue of the Christian college influence is more obvious. What do you make of the fact that those who attend college and graduate are more inclined to still be in church as adults compared to those who do not enroll in college or those who do and fail to graduate? Here is a possible explanation. The first exam that I took in college was a biology test. I failed with a grade somewhere around 64 or so. I was in shock. I did not make the best grades in high school and one thing I rarely did in my teen years was study. My failing grade was a wake-up call. It did not make me want to quit. The failure made me more determined. I committed to make a correction and adjust my approach. I did not graduate with honors but I did make the adjustments that allowed me to graduate with a degree in four years. In addition, as my maturity developed, I went on to get a masters and doctorate with the highest marks possible.

The point of sharing my journey is not to boast because I got off to a very rough start in college academically, socially, and spiritually. However, my faith development as a teenager and the work of God in my life prompted me to grow in my commitment and to have a "never give up" attitude. Perhaps the deeper issue that is reflected by this finding has little to do with education and much to do with personal commitment and determination. Some people opt not to go to college because they have a skill, trade, or passion they want to develop. However, others choose not to go because they do not want to do the work. Some start and do not finish the task because the work is too hard. They give up. Do not feel insulted if you never graduated college because I am speaking broadly at this point and you would not be reading this if you were not a person of commitment yourself. However, it is a reality that a strong sense of commitment is required to get an academic degree.

One of my daughters played basketball when she was about ten years of age. It was her second season and though she was not skilled, she likely played because I, her father, enjoyed basketball. I did not compel her to play but was excited that we shared this common interest. However, she got frustrated and announced that she was going to quit about half way through the season. What does a parent do at this point? Here is how I responded: "No you are not going to quit. You may choose not to play next year but you signed up and made a commitment. You will go to every practice and to every game and give it your best. We do not quit in this family! Ever! Do you understand?" She was not happy and cried as ten-year-old girls are prone to do. Do you know what else she did? She fulfilled her commitment. She may not remember that experience but those types of moments stick with a child. I wish you could spend some time with her now. As an adult, I have seen her face some obstacles with bulldog determination and overcome challenges that would cause many to quit. If the Holy Spirit indwells us as believers, we should have an attitude of perseverance and commitment like that modeled by Jesus when He endured the cross.

A Word for Parents

College for your child is *an* issue but it is not *the* issue. What are you teaching your child about commitment? Why do some young adults who grow up in church remain in church as adults? They are committed to their faith. They are committed to whatever the task is that they encounter. What you teach about commitment is important. What you model for them is imperative. Do you have a "no quit" attitude? Is it reflected in your church life, family life, and work life?

You should know that if you attend church, you will eventually get your feelings hurt. Someone will let you down. You will get upset with someone somewhere along the line. A pastor or leader may make a mistake that offends or bothers you. The church is filled with flawed people and imperfect leaders. Perhaps you have already experienced something like this. I know of many who have been hurt and opted to quit. They stop serving and stop attending. Then years later, they wonder why their children are not strong in their faith.

What if you have already quit? In that case you need to re-commit. Start from where you are and determine to model what it means to be committed to Jesus Christ and to be devoted to the body of Christ, the church. First and foremost, you do not need to recommit for your child. You need to recommit for your Savior. Remember that the church was not man's idea. Jesus is the one who established the church. Perhaps you do not feel you need the church. However, the church needs you. It is not the building or the organization that I am referring to. It is the people. Whether you realize it or not, you also need them. If not now, the time will come. When you came to faith in Jesus, he gave you spiritual gifts. The purpose of these gifts is to enable you to strengthen the body, the church. You cannot be both disconnected from the body and strengthen the body any more than my hand can serve me if it is cut off. Your connection to the church or lack thereof is sending a message to your child. How much do you love Jesus Christ? Do you love His body? Do you love His bride? What do you communicate when you say you love Christ but are not connected to His church? And remember this: it is never too late to do what is right, but the sooner the better.

Regarding college, perhaps you will give your child options as I did with mine. Tuition, housing, scholarships, degree programs, size of the school, the location, and affection for certain institutions are all factors that influence the decision of where to attend. Be sure to place Christian colleges on the list and encourage your child to give it strong consideration. Whether you expect your child to attend college or not, be sure to read on into Chapter Nineteen to learn something else that is critical to keeping your child in church into their adult years.

A Word for Pastors

You can begin by sharing this information with parents. Do so through your counseling, as you engage in conversation, and through your preaching. The chapters you are reading that reflect on the college experience are not subjects your parents should be hearing for the first time after their children move off to college. Parents of preschoolers and children need to hear this in advance as well as those who have teens who are soon destined for graduation from high school. Remember also the root issue that has been discussed. Teach families about commitment. What does it mean to be committed? What does the Bible teach? How does commitment affect our marriages, our families, and the faith of our children? My personal approach is to exhort those who I lead. I do not want to "beat them up" with an issue, but to encourage them to personal growth and deeper commitment. It must begin with me and in your church it must begin with you.

Consider what you might do to assist with helping families make good decisions about which college the students in your church will attend. Recruiters or students from Christian colleges would be delighted to attend your church to meet with students and parents. You might consider a small college fair with a special invitation to the Christian colleges from your state and those that are within a few hours' drive. If you have a smaller group of students, consider taking them to a college fair. You could accomplish several tasks with this approach, the greatest of which may be in deepening your personal relationship with the high school students.

College matters, but more importantly, commitment matters. The next chapter will reveal a significant point that all pastors and churches need to address. Although students graduate from high school, we should not treat them as if they have graduated from our church and from our influence. When students graduate from high school, the church should not treat them as if they have completed something, though we certainly should celebrate their accomplishments. The church should treat high school grads as if they are beginning something, and the next four to six years are critical in their faith development. The research revealed that proactivity by parents, pastors, and church leaders with college age young adults has a significant influence over whether those who grew up in church will continue to attend and serve as adults. Do not stop investing following high school graduation for your students. Now is the time to ramp it up rather than back it down. Get to it!

QUESTIONS FOR DISCUSSION

1. How can your church assist those who choose not to attend college to continue to grow in their faith?
2. What does your church do to help families with making decisions about college for students who attend the church? What can be done to assist in the future?
3. Why do you think there is such a strong correlation in North America between a student attending and graduating from college and the likelihood that he/she stay in church as adults for those who grew up attending church?

CHAPTER NINETEEN

HAVE YOU FOUND A GOOD CHURCH?

Tom Crites

"Too cold for just my jean jacket," he thought to himself as he left the radio station late one afternoon. But it was his only option for the long walk back to campus. The college student did his best to pull the jacket tight around his shoulders as he started the journey. It was an interesting time in his life as he was finishing up his senior year; an opportunity to intern at a local country music radio station allowed him to get a sample of the "real world." But it did not take long to see that the real world tasted somewhat bittersweet. The realities of hard choices were weighing heavy on him now, only a few weeks after selling his car to help cover the costs of his education. The noble idea of having to "rough it" seemed to fade as the brisk wind caused the shivers to climb up his back. Just before he really started feeling sorry for himself, an extended cab pickup slowed and a passenger side window was lowered. "Do you need a ride?" a fifty-something lady offered the verbal lifeline with her husband patiently idling. "I really do," said the young traveler as he reached for the back seat door handle. "Thank you so much!" The conversation and experience that followed made a tremendous impact on the young man *and* on the good Samaritans that night.

The young man who faced a long walk back to campus that chilly evening was actually me. I was thrilled to have been shown grace by this incredible caring couple. We chatted about my studies and about being a student at Union University. They shared about their daughter, a recent Union graduate, and their positive experiences with the school. Then they took a stab at deepening our connection when they asked, "Would you like to come with us to our Wednesday night dinner at church? That is where we were heading when we stopped to pick you up." That invitation and my hesitant response to dinner that night would make a huge difference in the life of this college student and those empty-nesters. I was the only college age person in the room that night but the atmosphere was positive and welcoming. I enjoyed the free meal, especially since only cold pizza or a bowl of Fruity Pebbles waited for me in my empty dorm room. And deep down, it refreshed my spirit to know that somebody cared about me, an anonymous college kid. In the weeks following, I enjoyed many of those free Wednesday night dinners and looked forward to the time that I had with my surrogate church family. By the time my brother attended Union only a few years later, West Jackson Baptist Church had developed a strong ministry to college students. The church had become a church home-away-from-home for hundreds of college kids. I like to think that a shivering college kid in a jean jacket had something to do with it, but the reality is that God had been working on the leaders of that church long before I ever met that kind couple.

The church sat within a short distance of the college for years, but no real connections existed. Former pastors attempted to reach the students, but nothing seemed to develop and soon efforts to minister to the college population were forsaken. The current pastor saw the need for a ministry directed toward the college students as well. He was just waiting for the right moment—the right connection. I don't know if my connection was the moment that "clicked" for the folks in that church, but soon after, the ministry to college students seemed to take off.

Churches like West Jackson are crucial to the spiritual health of young adults. Our research revealed that a young adult who is connected with a congregation quickly after high school is 138% more likely to stay in church than the young adult who does not connect with a church in the transition time after high school. As Steve discussed in the preceding chapters, not every young adult experiences this transition time while in college. Some young adults join the military and some immediately enter the workforce, but wherever the transition takes place, this is a critical period in the spiritual life of a young adult.

In Chapter Eighteen, Steve revealed that when young adults were asked, "What do you think the church thinks about you?" their answers were basically, "They don't take us seriously," or "They don't think about us at all." It is a real shame that many young adults hold those perceptions. When we reviewed the literature that focused on the issue of young adults leaving the church, the sources unanimously identified a "big gap" or "black hole" in people's spiritual development. We saw the same gap: young adults stray from church in the few years between high school and marriage. No wonder we have dedicated three full chapters and part of a fourth to the issues directly related to this stage of life. It is important that Christians be aware and prepared to assist our children, grandchildren, relatives, and friends as they navigate some of the most difficult years they will face. Let's examine several pieces to the puzzle that reveal some practical things we can do to help young adults stay in church through this important transition in life.

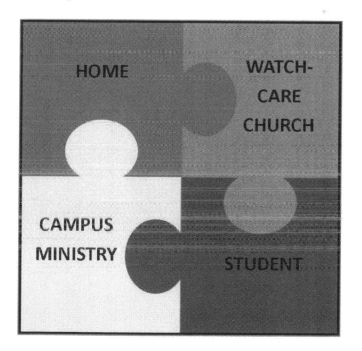

Puzzle Piece 1–The Home and Home Church

As you read, our research showed a strong correlation between those who stayed and a college aged focused ministry in the church that they call their home church. I want to implore our churches, no matter what size, whether a college is in your town or 100 miles away, to strongly consider developing a ministry to college aged individuals. A youth pastor or youth worker, or even a parent, may have to take the lead in reaching out to this group. There is a natural flow of relationship that has been nurtured while the student has grown up in the youth ministry. It only makes sense that this relationship is continued.

We cannot wash our hands of our students when they go away to college or join the military; it remains the home church's responsibility until they connect after their move. With that in mind we need to begin laying the foundation for church connection before the student graduates high school. What have we done for our students to help them connect? Reread Chapter Eighteen to gather some practical ideas for a local pastor. But also recruit someone to become the "college connection" leader. As the college connection leader, he/she will work to maintain a connection with each college age young adult after they have moved away. He/she can factor in some accountability, not in a negative, hounding type of approach, but in an encouraging way to ask how things are going with finding a new church. This person can also head up the efforts to send care packages, cards, and notes to encourage the young person as they face new and sometimes challenging moments in life. The college connection leader can ask individuals to pray for the young person while they are away, asking the Lord to protect and provide.

Puzzle Piece 2–The Watch-Care Church

In the past few years, the U.S. has had about 6% of the population enrolled in higher education, which equals about 19 million people. There are literally thousands of colleges, universities, trade schools, and community colleges dotting our landscape.[34] Except for the most extreme situations, it would not surprise me if every person reading this book were within a twenty-mile drive to an institution of higher learning. And if you are one of those who are not within twenty miles, you probably have hundreds of college students within twenty miles of your church taking online classes. I mention those stats to make a point: we have military bases, colleges, and college age students all around us. These young adults need local churches.

I have seen churches effectively minister to college age young adults by developing a watch-care ministry (or something similar with a different name). This is a ministry that is organized by a local church to "adopt" college students or military personnel who are temporarily in their neighborhood. A church will assign a family or a couple of individual volunteers to a student whom they can invite to church functions, family get-togethers, or whatever may be happening in the watch-care church family. This watch-care family becomes a connection to a student who is away from home. This ministry is particularly important to the international students at a local college. These students do not travel home often, if at all, during their education in the U.S., so they are in the neighborhood for every break and holiday. Most schools require these students to vacate the dorms during breaks so they are looking for places to stay during the holidays. They long to have time with a "family," as theirs may be thousands of miles away. They may celebrate Christmas or Easter for the first time in the home of a watch-care family. They will no doubt have access to the gospel as people open their homes to the needs of these students. In addition, when and if your influence results in an international student coming to faith in Jesus Christ, they will take their faith with them back to their home country. Catch that vision. You could impact international missions by reaching out to these students throughout the year.

While international students are in need of watch-care families, so are the "not-so-local" students. These students are far enough away from home that they do not go home every weekend, and are close enough to home that they do go home for breaks and holidays. They need a watch-care family to help them remain connected to the local church. They may need a family to share Sunday dinner or an opportunity to do a load of laundry. Sometimes they need a quiet place to get away and study or even rest. A watch-care family can be all these things for college age young adults.

Consider the watch-care opportunities around the church. Are there colleges or military bases nearby? Are there factories with a number of semi-migrant employees from out of state or out of country? Is there another opportunity to offer watch-care type ministry? Creating a watch-care ministry in your church may help a young adult keep a connection to church during this incredibly important time in his spiritual development.

Puzzle Piece 3–The College Based Ministry

A good collegiate ministry is vital to the spiritual maturity of a young believer. It can help connect students to churches by training churches and associations in the development of their collegiate ministries. Then they can provide opportunities throughout the year for students to become aware of churches that are interested in involving and ministering to collegians. Campus ministers are available to assist churches in identifying students (and sometimes student teams) who are gifted in music, drama, sign language, retreat leadership, preaching, speaking, and other skills.

Campus ministries facilitate connections between local churches through opportunities like mission trips where students obtain valuable ministry experiences. The students will be able to draw from those experiences in missions that will positively impact the Kingdom of God in the churches they join in the future. Students are an almost inexhaustible source of energy for regional mission projects, neighborhood outreach events, and church ministries. Students keep going and going long after old guys like me give out.

Campus ministers help create an environment that encourages committed Christians to live what they believe, and challenges them to become leaders. They help college age students stretch and grow in their faith. The campus minister can facilitate opportunities for the students to exercise their gifts in a group. They challenge the believer to reach out to the campus to share the gospel with unbelieving peers. In many ways, a good collegiate ministry reflects a good youth ministry at a local church. But it is so much more, and should be.

Puzzle Piece 4–The Young Adult

Yes, the young adult has to take some responsibility for the connection as well. I remember a big joke that went around while I was in college;

a person who overslept or slept in on Sunday said they attended "Bed Springs Baptist." Some may have even had perfect attendance at Bed Springs! I know how things are. I personally have two college age children in my family, and they love to sleep in. We have to remember that Jesus gave the *church* the Great Commission; there is no plan "B." There never needs to be a moment in our lives when we are disconnected from the church. When you are exclusively attending the local campus ministry you are missing out on the interaction with senior adults, other adults, and children in Christ's body. Those of us in ministry know the benefit of being around older, wiser Christians. We also know the blessings that come with serving and mentoring others. This is the perfect time in a person's life to begin serving the body as well as receiving ministry from the body.

In summary, the student's family and home church is encouraging the connection. The watch-care church is providing ministry for the connection. The campus ministry is facilitating the connection. And finally, the student is receiving the connection.

A Word for Pastors

If you have not started to think about how you can minister to college age young adults, you need to do so now. Look around your community for the opportunities to minister to young people who are away from their homes. Look with a "yes we can" attitude not a "we can't do it" attitude. Remember, sometimes the smallest, seemingly insignificant moments can make a tremendous difference in the lives of local students and our church members.

In addition, take the initiative with those high school students who are members of your congregation as they graduate each fall. Get their cell phone numbers and call them a few times in September, October, and November after they move away to college, the military, or to work in another community. You can do this yourself if the congregation is small and the number of graduates is few in number. If the number is larger, take the initiative to get someone else involved. If the church is large, you may need to enlist a team. Remember, your task is not complete upon high school graduation. Making contact to encourage, ask about church, invite them back when they're home for the holidays, or recommend a church, provides a level of accountability that most young adults are not receiving from their home churches. Finally, make a fuss over them when they are home, in a way that is affirming. You are a major influence and these first months away are critical. When you help them make the transition, the church will benefit for years to come.

A Word for Parents

Take it upon yourself to help your college age young adult find a church where they can connect while they are away from home. This may take a few calls, notes of encouragement, and weekend visits where you attend a local church together to encourage your student to become connected. Find a way to lovingly guide them toward becoming involved. It would not hurt to talk to them about the "big gap" in church attendance for college students and how they may be 138% more likely to stay involved if they remain connected to a church.

QUESTIONS FOR DISCUSSION

1. What does your church do to help students who attend college away from home to connect with a local church?
2. What does your church do to help local college students and military personnel (or others) become connected to your church?
3. What are three practical ideas that your church can utilize to help improve the chances of students connecting to your local church?

CHAPTER TWENTY

THE BIBLE TELLS ME SO

Tom Crites

S tanding on the porch of the church each morning of Vacation
Bible School week was a nerve-wracking experience for a ten-
year-old. It wasn't the energy swell that grew from the continuous
stream of sugar coated cereal-eating kids emerging from station
wagon after station wagon, darting here and there on the small patchy
church lawn. It wasn't the well-intended volunteer grandma who
tried to exercise crowd control by randomly puffing a whistle in the
direction of the boys getting too near the parking lot. It wasn't even
the anticipation of the day's events that would surely include lots of
laughs and good times with my friends. What caused the butterflies
to awaken in my stomach each of those five days in June was the
possibility of being selected to carry the American Flag, the Christian
flag, or the Bible during the VBS processional. Yeah, yeah, I know that
doesn't seem that exciting to you, but as a ten-year-old kid who spent
the summer goofing around, having the honor of leading the VBS
herd by carrying one of those three items was of utmost importance
during the fifteen minutes before a normal VBS day. Every VBS
veteran knew that if you wanted to be selected for the duty, you had to
arrive early enough to gather on the porch, strategically peek through
the front window and look longingly (but not too desperately) to the
teenager selecting the day's representatives. If you were lucky, you
would be selected to lead the important opening moments of VBS.

Okay, all kidding aside, I recall the way VBS started every day. We said the pledges—first to the American flag, then to the Christian flag, and then to the Bible. Do you remember the words of those pledges? I do. Of course we all recall and continue to recite the pledge to the American flag, but we seldom recite the pledges to the Christian flag or the Bible. The pledge to the Bible goes like this: "I pledge allegiance to the Bible, God's Holy Word, and will make it a lamp unto my feet, a light unto my path, and hide its Word in my heart that I may not sin against God." I did not understand what I was pledging back in my elementary years, but later in life, I had to decide if I would keep my allegiance to the Bible. Every person has to determine if he or she will stay true to the Bible or if there will be other standards that will guide his/her decisions.

The decision to look to the Bible as light for my path came easier to me than perhaps to some others. It was directly related to that VBS Bible pledge—not only that pledge, but the number of times that I heard and saw my Sunday School teachers, my pastor, and my parents communicate that I could believe and trust the Bible as God's Holy Word. This high view of Scripture was planted early in my spiritual formation. As I grew, my assurance of the sufficiency of God's Word grew and blossomed. When I finally faced the challenge of a secular humanistic view, I was able to stand firmly by my convictions because I truly believed that the Bible is the Holy Word of God.

The participants in our survey shared their feelings about Scripture and an important factor was identified. Those who stayed in church had a higher view of Scripture than those who strayed from church. As a matter of fact, they were 25 times more likely to have strayed if they had a low view of Scripture. Those who shared that they had a "high" to "very high" view of Scripture were 84% more likely to have stayed connected to church. When asked an open-ended question about why they stayed in church or why they strayed from church, the third most common self-described reason of those who strayed was related to "intellectual doubts." You are probably not surprised by these results. Frankly, they did not surprise me either, but I was surprised by the size of the gap identified by those who stayed and those who strayed. When I was a young man in college and seminary, the battle for the Bible was raging. Major denominations wrestled with the issues of inerrancy and biblical dependability. The battle seemed to have been won in the halls of the denominations and that is good in my opinion but, culturally, the battle for the Bible is being lost. Pragmatism is driving church life in response to a culture that does not believe the Bible is truly the Word of God. As a result, young people are disconnecting from churches and finding their needs met in other communities that feel, to them, as relevant as a church. As a leader of a major denomination, I feel ashamed that we have rested on the laurels of winning the "battle for the Bible" yet we are losing the hearts of our young people. The issue of biblical sufficiency is a major issue in the lives of our next generation.

A Word for Pastors

You are in a war! The Evil One roams the highways seeking to devour the souls of your young people. These children are entrusted to your care. You must protect them. As the shepherd of these people, I encourage you to lead your congregation to adopt a high view of Scripture. Challenge them to believe the Bible has the answers and then provide them with resources and teaching that will solidify that position in their hearts. Teach the children in your church to honor God's Word. Teach the youth the doctrines of the faith. Teach the adults how to handle doubts about the Bible. Train yourself in apologetics so that when a member comes to you with a question, you will be ready to respond.

The teens in your congregation will be challenged when they attend college and as other influences infiltrate their lives. Much like the house in Matthew chapter seven that experienced storms, winds, and floods, the foundation on which they stand will make a difference. Give them the tools they need to depend on the Word of God. Do not be afraid to teach apologetics and theology to your younger members. If they do not receive the instruction from you then they will find it from other sources. Will the other sources support a higher view of Scripture?

How can they trust God's Word as being inspired by the Holy Spirit and applicable to their lives today? What are the proofs of the resurrection? Can science and the Bible co-exist and maintain credibility on both parts? Are the translations of the Bible throughout time reliable? How do we know Jesus really existed? This list is far from exhaustive. It is not enough to simply say that they should believe because you believe. Many great resources are available and you need to put these in the hands of teens well before graduation day.

A practical thing that you can do right now is to develop a library of resources available to your members for checkout. Ask some of your pastor friends what resources they would recommend. Be sure to find resources appropriate for different age levels. After you have time to plan, put together a training event or class that will inform and train your members. They will appreciate the help and grow in their faith.

A Word for Parents

Do your children see you reading your Bible? Have they heard you read it to them? Have they heard you tell them what you have recently learned from the Bible or how something you read has impacted your life? If not, then you have not been teaching them the value of the Bible.

A pastor friend of mine shared how after his mother died, the five children split a small inheritance and he was stunned by how small the amount of the check equaled. But then he remembered that his parents left him a better inheritance. They taught him to love the Lord and to love His Word. To him, that was a precious treasure more valuable than any amount of gold or silver. Teach your children to love and trust the Bible. Remember what the Psalmist wrote in Psalm 119:105, *Your Word is a lamp to my feet and a light for my path* (HCSB). God's Word is a light in every corner of the darkness that your children might face. Equip them with the tool that will help them navigate all their ways.

QUESTIONS FOR DISCUSSION

1. What are the greatest challenges children in your church will face concerning the sufficiency of the Bible?
2. How did your parents and/or grandparents demonstrate that they had a high view of Scripture? How did that impact your faith?
3. In what ways does your church encourage a high view of Scripture? How can this be improved or built upon?
4. What resources have you found helpful in answering the difficult questions that our culture presents concerning the value of the Bible?

CHAPTER TWENTY-ONE

GROW ON NOW

Tom Crites

"You popped the clutch," my dad repeated, getting a bit irritated at my inability to pull out of the Walmart parking lot. "Ugh!" I expressed, after hearing the brief explanation of my failure for the tenth time. I anxiously looked at the oncoming traffic, beyond embarrassed, and observed the growing number of vehicles lining up behind me. My glance desperately searched the right then the left looking for another opening that might provide my escape from this torture. My chance came, and then went with another lunge forward and another engine stall. I jerked the emergency brake up and flung open the car door. "I can't do it!" Defeated, I walked the shameful ten steps around to the passenger side and slumped into the seat, squeezing my eyes tightly to avoid eye contact with any witness to my drama.

Still steaming, I was delivered home in silence by my very patient father. I entered my home and announced to the world that I would never be able to drive a stick shift. After two weeks of mental anguish, I agreed to an invitation from my dad to try again, who suggested that we practice in the Kroger parking lot until I got it. And, to my surprise, after about thirty minutes of trial and error, I was able to propel the car without the sudden jerk and stall that I had painfully grown accustomed to in my previous experience. My fifteen-year-old life was spared the pressure of being a permit-only driver, and the day after I turned sixteen, I successfully passed my driver's exam in the same car that I had experienced such monumental failure just a few months earlier. Had it not been for the encouragement and instruction given by my family and my personal commitment to face the challenge, I may have thumbed rides for years before accomplishing the goal of becoming a driver of the intimidating stick shift.

While the commitment to learn to drive a stick shift pales in comparison to the commitment to grow in a relationship with the Lord, some of the principles do relate. I had to come to the place where I wanted to conquer the stick shift and understand that I could not give up when I seemed to have failed. Even in the failure, I learned more about the process. I needed the encouragement and help from my father, who had been driving a stick shift for years. I needed to know that everyone has challenges learning to drive—some more than others, but everyone pops the clutch every now and then.

What does all of this have to do with why young people stay in church? I'm glad you asked. Commitment is a real issue for young adults. Those who have stayed in church communicated to us that they made a personal commitment to grow in their faith. In fact, a young person staying in church was 71% more likely to say that a "personal" commitment was important to them. No one made, imposed, or conferred commitment upon them. While parents, family, friends, and church leaders had an influence on them, their faith became rooted in a personal experience with Jesus Christ.

I recently had the opportunity to sit down with a group of young adults to ask them about personal commitment. I uncovered some interesting perspectives to consider for those who stayed connected to the church. First, the commitment young adults wanted to talk about is what separates a nominal Christian or a cultural Christian from a devoted Christian. A nominal Christian may claim a connection to a church or religious group just to avoid an uncomfortable discussion. Many nominal Christians in the neighborhood around my church that I invited to attend worship or asked them about their faith mentioned that they grew up Baptist (or Methodist, Catholic, Pentecostal, or whatever) hoping that I would not dig deeper into their spiritual life. Nominalism is a real issue. A recent study of world religion estimated that 1.2 billion people are nominal Christians.[35] The sad tragedy of nominal Christians is that they are not engaged beyond verbal acknowledgement. They may sporadically attend a local church but do not serve, share their faith, engage in missions, or impact their community. You might not even know they are connected to a church or claim to be a Christian unless you pin them down on the subject.

Similarly, a cultural Christian finds himself equipped with the vocabulary of faith but is actually on the outside looking in. A cultural Christian is at least the second generation of a string of relatives or friends who are genuine believers. These kinds of people have been around the church long enough to be familiar with its customs and beliefs, but they have never internalized them. They may even enjoy practicing the sacraments or traditions and may be found at church on many occasions though they are not likely to serve or exercise any of the spiritual disciplines apart from occasional participation in some church activities. Let me say something here: I am not judging any particular person. I cannot know if a person has truly trusted Christ for salvation or not; only God knows that. I am making a judgment on a "type." A nominal or cultural Christian may be a believer (which is why I chose to use the terms containing the word "Christian"). They may be far from God, running from God, or experiencing doubts and thus not acting very Christ-like. Or they may even attend church frequently, wear the right clothes, say the right things, and do some good deeds, but be just as far away from God. What is most important to see within this discussion is the fact that young adults who stay in church do not fit this profile.

The Christianity that the group of young adults wanted to talk about was a personal faith. They each had a moment when the faith of their fathers, or their culture, became their personal faith in Jesus Christ. I asked them if they were talking about the moment they became a Christian and each of them responded, "No, it was another moment." What they described was a moment of "taking hold" of their call to be set apart or consecrated. They made a personal commitment to grow in their faith. When they made the commitment to grow in a personal relationship with Jesus, everything changed. One described the experience of "stepping into the sunlight out of a perfectly lighted room." He was able to see things clearly and understand things more fully now that his faith was becoming "real." They were expressing the fruit of a life that had been positively impacted and encouraged to follow Christ, and they were identifying an important factor related to the reasons why young adults stay in church.

You may want to reference Chapter Eighteen again at this point, where Steve connected this issue of commitment to the strength of faith of those who grow up and then stay in church. Everything discussed in this book is designed to help you create an environment where the children and teens in your family and church can come to a point of personal commitment to growth and faith in Jesus Christ. Parents and pastors cannot make the commitment for the next generation. Your responsibility is to do all that you can to provide the best possible environment for growth in faith to take place. You sow the seeds and pray that God will help the commitment to take root. However, in addition to sowing the seeds, you prepare the soil of their hearts much like a farmer plows and prepares the ground before he sows his crop. Take all of the preceding issues and do all you can to make sure they are true in the lives of those for whom you have responsibility. Personal commitment to Christ is most likely to stream out of the environment that you have been learning more about.

We have concluded previous chapters with words for pastors and for parents. As this section of the book comes to an end, the previous fourteen chapters will suffice for advice on how to provide an environment that leads a child or adolescent to a personal commitment to grow in their faith. However, do not be afraid to call teens to commitment in your church. Do not manipulate, coerce, or assume the commitment is there. But on the other hand, do not hesitate to occasionally call for commitment. The Lord may use those opportunities to call some to ministry, to missions, or simply to deeper devotion to Jesus Christ.

Finally, as devoted Christian parents, we all desire that our children make such a commitment to grow in their faith. Parenting them can be a harrowing journey as we worry about where they will land with their personal level of commitment. Be faithful and trust that God will work. Sometimes you will be blessed, as I was sometime back, with a glimmer of encouragement.

I remember when my son was a junior in high school. He and his friends asked if they could have an after prom get-together at our home, beginning at 11:00 p.m.! I asked lots of questions and found that this "party" had a name—Kingdom Culture—and this event had a purpose: to give the kids an alternative to the other after prom options. I found out that the party would be over at 2:00 (yes, in the morning) and that after the party, the girls were retreating to a neighbor's house and the guys were crashing at our house. I also discovered that Kingdom Culture involved fifty, I repeat *fifty*, kids planning to attend. My wife and I cautiously agreed to host Kingdom Culture. We warned the neighbors—which became a testimony in itself—prepared our basement for the party, and held on for dear life. It was amazing! I sat upstairs in my recliner listening to fifty teens sing praise and worship until the wee hours of the morning. The next day I saw where they had taken time to pray, writing out prayer requests on the backs of paper bags. They wrote testimonies of God's faithfulness and tacked them to the walls. It was beautiful and it was all *their* doing. I have to admit, I was really worried about that evening. I did not want to be kept up until way after my bedtime. However, God really got a hold of many of those kids that night. I thank God for moments like these as a parent and pray that you and I will both have many similar experiences as we pass our faith on to the next generation.

QUESTIONS FOR DISCUSSION

1. Share when you felt that you took the next step in your faith. When did it become personal for you?
2. What are some ways that your church encourages young people in their spiritual formation?
3. What are some resources that you have found to be helpful in your devotional life that you could share with a young person to encourage spiritual growth?

PART THREE
MORE TO THE STORY

CHAPTER TWENTY-TWO

WORK TO DO

Steve Parr

The phone rang and the person who answered quickly recognized that his doctor was on the line. "I have good news and bad news," the doctor began. "Which do you want first?"

"Give me the good news first," his patient replied.

"The good news is that you have three days to live."

"That's the good news? Then what in the world is the bad news?"

"I've been trying to call you for the last two days!"

So far you have been exposed to good news and bad news. The bad news is that the church is losing too many young adults and the gap where they fall through the crack is the widest during the three to six years following high school graduation. The good news is that of the fifteen issues discussed in the previous section, fourteen can be directly addressed and improved upon in tangible ways. The only factor we have discussed so far over which you have no control is the temperament of a child growing up. But now you know that if your child is very strong willed you better be extra attentive to the other fourteen issues in order to maximize the probability that they will stay in church into their adult lives.

The fifteen critical issues broke down broadly as follows:

- Four related to the **parenting** received while growing up. (Chapters 9, 11, 12, 16)

- Four related in some way to a person's **discipleship experience** while growing up. (Chapters 7, 8, 20, 21)
- Three related in some way to a person's **church experience** while growing up. (Chapters 13, 14, 15)
- Three related to a person's immediate **post high school experience**. (Chapters 17, 18, 19)
- One related to a person's **temperament** as a child. (Chapter 10)

You will note that the key issue is in bold print and the related chapters are included with each grouping. Often upon attending a conference or reading a book you can feel a bit overwhelmed by the information. Though this chapter is brief, it is intended to assist you in assimilating the information shared to this point so that you can process what you have learned and begin to place your focus where it can make the greatest difference.

The preceding list can help you as a parent or a church leader to broadly understand issues that need to be addressed and strategies that need to be developed. Attention should be given to improving marriages and parenting, to providing a healthy church environment, to providing a more effective discipleship experience for children, teens, and younger adults, and to maintaining a connection that helps older teens navigate their post high school years. You have plenty of work to do here with what you have learned so far but there is more to the story.

It is important that you understand that none of the issues that have been studied so far work in isolation. They each work in combination and in harmony with the others. I conducted a study a few years back of the fastest growing churches in our state and identified ten common traits. Not all of the churches shared every one of the ten traits. However, each church shared an average of nine of the ten traits. A random follow-up study revealed that other growing churches, though not the fastest growing, averaged eight of the ten traits. However, those that were not growing typically shared fewer than five of the traits.

The point is that not all fifteen of the issues discovered will likely apply to any individual, but if they do you can be assured that he or she is currently serving in a local church somewhere. On the other hand, if only one of the traits is true for an individual, it is highly unlikely that he or she attends church today. We do not live in a perfect world, and fitting all fifteen characteristics around the development of a child may seem impossible. But do not give up because if you can implement or apply circumstances that result in a majority of the traits being true for the child over whom you have influence, the glue that holds them in church will be very strong.

Moving forward you will learn that some of the fifteen issues, when combined together, can serve as spiritual super glue that can keep your children connected into their adult years. No guarantees are possible but the probabilities skyrocket when some of the fifteen are prioritized and applied effectively.

In addition, you will discover ten other issues that make some difference. The variation is not as great as what you have studied so far, but each one had a notable influence. These will be addressed briefly so that you can do all that is possible to invest in the lives of the children and teens over which you have responsibility. I assume you want to do everything in your power to make the greatest difference possible. Your leadership is impressive to me in that you have read this far. Do not stop here. Read on so that you can make an impact that will last for years and into eternity.

QUESTIONS FOR DISCUSSION

1. What has been the greatest takeaway for you to this point?
2. Based on what you have learned so far, what is the greatest concern that you have for your children or for those children who are under your leadership at your church?
3. Choose a child in your family or one who attends your church. Go through the fifteen issues and determine how many are true for the child at this point. How does it look? Of one issue over which you have influence, what action should you begin to take to help bolster their discipleship experience?

CHAPTER TWENTY-THREE

PARENTS OR THE PARISH:
WHAT MATTERS MOST?

Tom Crites

"As long as you live under my roof, you will live by my rules!" I heard my father say passionately to my brother as I quietly closed my bedroom door to shield my ears from the loud argument taking place in the other room. My stomach churned and knotted at the emotional outbursts, seemingly getting tighter with every verbal volley. I hoped the confrontation would soon be over, as the seconds seemed like years. Tears of pain and relief escaped out of the sides of my eyes as a slammed door and screeching tires leaving the driveway punctuated the argument. The house became exceedingly silent. I let out a deep sigh, sort of cleansing my atmosphere that had been disturbed by the release of what seemed like toxic fumes. Again, my heart hurt for my parents and my brother as they wrestled through his transition into adulthood.

My brother was a very strong-willed kid. Steve shared about the challenges of parents with strong-willed kids in Chapter Ten. I encourage you to keep that chapter handy as you navigate your parenting challenges. In retrospect, I see that my parents knew the only way they were going to survive the strong-willed teenage years was a steady, firm commitment to their values. They knew that they could not budge on the rules as they were setting the standard for the whole family. Consistency was to be one of the most important things observed from my parents as they raised three demanding kids. I never doubted where my parents stood morally, as they clearly demonstrated and verbalized their boundaries for our family. Even though my brother (and eventually I) tried to push their boundaries, they remained firm in their faith and everything that it meant.

In our research, we discovered young adults were most likely to stay in church if their parents modeled strong faith. As a matter of fact, using a factor analysis to evaluate the data, a strong faith variable scored significantly higher than any other factors identified. It was clear that the parents (or a parent) who modeled a strong faith impacted their young adult's decision to stay in church. We have touched on several important points in the earlier chapters of this book, but considering them as a cluster will help you see the importance of this issue.

The analysis revealed that there was a strong relationship between two groupings of variables and the decision to stay in church. The first group focused on the young adults' perceptions of their parents' relationship to God. Consider the illustration below:

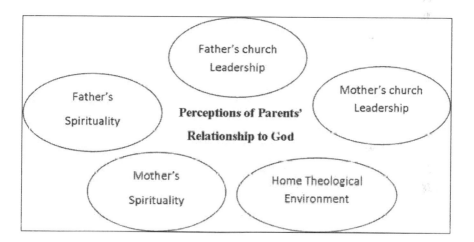

When young adults were asked the following questions, the way they answered revealed the relationship. They were asked, "Which role would best characterize your father's leadership in the church when you were growing up?" This related to another question: "Which would best characterize your mother's spirituality while you were living at home?" Together those related to three others: (1) "Which of these would best characterize the theological environment of your home growing up?" (2) "Which role would best characterize your mother's leadership in the church when you were growing up?" and (3) "Which would best characterize your father's spirituality while you were living at home?" These five variables hovered around a young adult's perception of his/her parents' relationship to God. They were telling us that they were more likely to stay in church if they witnessed their parents living in a close relationship with the Lord. Together, these five clustered variables represent one of the main influences in keeping young adults in church. If parents model a close relationship to the Lord, it may be the **most influential thing** they can do to encourage their child to stay in church.

Another factor was identified as almost as important as modeling a close relationship to the Lord. The second group of variables focused on the young adults' perceptions of their parents' feelings about their church. View these variables below:

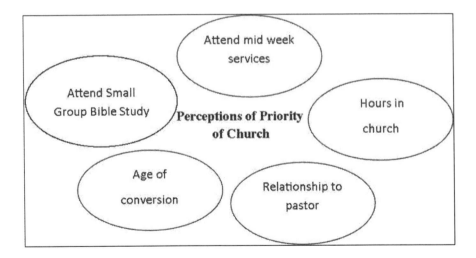

The questions that clustered to reveal the next major factor included: "Did you regularly attend mid-week services/activities during the majority of your years growing up?"; "How many hours did you typically spend in church services each week when you were in grades six through ten?"; "Did you regularly attend a small group such as Sunday School during the majority of your years growing up?"; "How old were you when you came into a relationship with Jesus Christ based on repentance of sin and faith in Jesus for salvation?" and "How would you characterize your relationship to your pastor while growing up?" These questions floated around the young adults' perceptions of the priority of church in their family life and revealed how their parents felt about church.

When considered together, it is easy to see the impact parents can make on a child when they live Godly lives and make church participation a priority in the home. Young adults come to understand that a close relationship lived within the context of local church participation is key to a happy life. While there are no guarantees regarding whether a child who grows up in church will continue as an adult, the research clearly revealed that as important as church experience is to those surveyed, the influence of the parents was of the greatest importance and sometimes navigated teens around bad church experiences. Stay connected. Stay faithful. But most of all, be what you desire your children to become.

QUESTIONS FOR DISCUSSION

1. How can parents sabotage their child's spiritual development through their church participation?
2. What are some things a parent can do to encourage a closer relationship between a child and his pastor?
3. What were some things that your parents did that demonstrated they were close to the Lord?

CHAPTER TWENTY-FOUR

LEVERAGING INFLUENCES

Steve Parr

M y senior year in high school was so much fun. My academic
coursework seemed to be easier and the schedule was lighter.
I went into both varsity sports that I played knowing that I would
definitely be a starter after doing likewise during my junior year. I
had a lot of friends, more freedom, a driver's license, and enough
dates to keep my young life interesting. The year was filled with lots
of fun and little responsibility. I was blessed to cap off my high school
experience with a happy senior year and graduation. It was fun to be
on top of the social totem pole.

Three months following graduation I was thrust from the top
to the bottom. I was a lowly freshman in college. My academic
coursework was unbelievably difficult, I had a full academic load,
I was not talented enough to play any college sport, I had few
friends initially on my new campus, and I had a total of two dates
in about nine months. I had even more freedom and still had my
driver's license, but that was about it. It did get better over time
but the first two months were especially difficult. Those were the
loneliest two months of my life to this point. The challenges also
affected me spiritually. I struggled for a brief season with my
commitment as I went through the transition from being a high
school somebody to a college freshman nobody. I did get through
it because of a good spiritual foundation, but the point is well

illustrated. Transitions are difficult and can be detrimental to one's faith development.

Parents and church leaders need to be especially attentive to three transitions that all North American adolescents will experience, and put extra energy into assisting teens through these common stages. They are as follows:

1. The transition from elementary to middle school; this ordinarily takes place when a child is about eleven to twelve years of age.
2. The transition from middle school to high school; this ordinarily takes place when a child is about fourteen to fifteen years of age.
3. The transition from high school to post-high school (college, military service, apprenticeship, or the work force); this ordinarily takes place when a young adult is about eighteen to nineteen years of age.

What do these transitions have in common? Though not an exhaustive list, here are some examples. In each circumstance the child or young adult goes from being the oldest and most mature among all of their peers to a new place where they are the youngest and often least mature. They often are moved to a new location or facility that is unfamiliar. They are more susceptible to being teased or bullied during the initial stages of the transition. It may mean they are placed with several if not many new peers that they will spend many hours with as well as being disconnected to some degree from former peers assigned to other places or groups.

To summarize with use of my earlier analogy, they go from being at the top of the social totem pole to the bottom. The drop to the bottom can be difficult, emotionally unsettling, and spiritually challenging. To make the new stage even more dramatic you factor in adolescence. The hormonal challenges, the onset of puberty, and the awkwardness of transforming from childhood to adult life can be unsettling enough even when the transitions are not added to the equation.

The research dramatized the potential influence of these evolutions in several ways. You may recall that the most likely time for a young person who grew up in church to disconnect was during the college years between about ages eighteen to twenty-three. Those years reflect perhaps the greatest transition of the three described previously. In addition, the value of a healthy youth ministry became crystal clear in the study. In the previous chapter you discovered the top cumulative effect on remaining active in church was by far the family model of spirituality. Notice that the second greatest collective grouping of factors was the church's influence on adolescence through youth ministry.

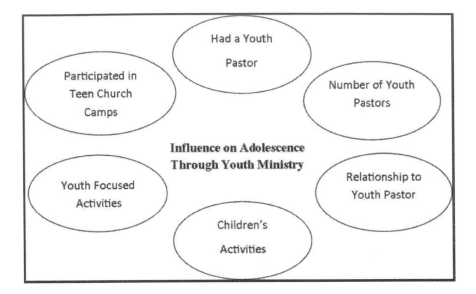

Here is a simple way to observe the value of a vibrant youth ministry in a church. A healthy youth ministry will tend to help parents and their children make the transition to middle school, high school, and then into post-high school life. An unhealthy youth ministry or the lack of a youth ministry altogether cannot serve as an asset to a parent or child during these critical transitions. You may recall from Chapter Five the discussion on guiding principles. You will find exceptions to everything, but the probabilities are greatly increased that a child who grows up in church will remain in church as an adult if certain factors are true in their life. The research revealed that those who attended churches with strong ministries to teens as well as targeted ministries to college age young adults were not just somewhat more inclined to remain in church as adults but were much more likely to have navigated all three of the transitions described and to still be active in the life of the church.

Here is a summary of some of the key points that relate:

- Whether one had a vocational youth pastor did not make a difference in whether one stayed in church, but whether they were part of a strong youth ministry did matter. Those who stayed in church as adults reflected that their church provided a "sufficient amount of youth activities" during their teen years, whereas those who had "strayed" stated that their church did not do likewise.
- For those who had a vocational youth pastor, the relationship was important. If they liked the youth pastor they were much more likely to be in church as an adult and if they did not like him or her they were much more likely to have "strayed."
- Having multiple youth pastors while growing up was detrimental.
- Attending church camps as a teen revealed a positive correlation between a person being in church as an adult.
- Having a "sufficient amount of children's activities" likewise had a positive correlation to those who "stayed."

To sum it all up, if a person growing up attended a church with a good children's ministry and a strong youth ministry, had a close relationship to one or more youth leaders, attended youth camps as a teen, and had minimal or no turnover in leadership during their high school years, he or she was very likely to still be involved in church as an adult when these factors were all combined and found to be true.

A Word for Pastors

Providing a healthy youth ministry in your church should not be viewed as an option but as essential to the discipleship of the teens in your congregation. A pastor does not have the luxury of neglecting any life stage group in the congregation or community. However, the teens are facing critical transitions that will affect their faith for a lifetime. In addition, most evangelistic opportunities are found among students. I am not suggesting that any life stage should be ignored, but I do suggest without apology that those who are ten to twenty years of age should be high priority.

You have three choices. First, you can do it yourself and if you lead a smaller congregation you may have to at first. Second, you can delegate it to someone else. Perhaps your church has resources to call a vocational youth pastor, but please be aware that other volunteers will still be critical for success. A skilled youth pastor can be a tremendous asset to congregations and families, but the study affirmed that volunteers can also make a great impact. Do you have a capable leader to whom the task can be delegated? The third option is to enlist a team and tackle this challenge together. You can be assured that parents will share your concerns.

Whatever you do, do not make excuses. You may say that this focus is not necessary because no teens attend your church. Why would they attend if there is no ministry for them? They are not adults and will not respond to a sign out front promoting the schedule of services. Adults must get involved in their lives to mentor, exhort, love, and challenge them to mature spiritually as well as physically, intellectually, and socially. Take a moment to read Luke 2:52 and see if this concept looks familiar.

Finally, work with parents and youth leaders to be strategic in helping teens and young adults with the three transitions. One of the ways that I did this as a youth pastor was to develop special activities and privileges available at each stage of their growth. The ministry I led made certain activities available only after a child reached the sixth grade. I have noticed some churches provide a dynamic ministry to children, with good intentions, and leave little if any new experiences for them to look forward to as middle school students. Provide special trips and activities that are only available once a child reaches sixth grade, others for those who reach ninth grade, others for those who are seniors in high school, and yet something else for the college age young adult. We would promote these opportunities for over a year prior to the transition and have the students anticipating and reaching with enthusiasm for the next level of their growth because of the "cool" trips, camps, weekends, or activities that were exclusive to the next stage of their growth. I hesitate to mention the specific activities because of cultural or generational differences but I hope the principle is clear.

A Word for Parents

I hope you are now more aware and better prepared as a result of knowing the challenges of these transitions. One key takeaway is the value of a strong youth ministry. How is it in your church? Do not wait until your child is in the sixth or seventh grade to notice. You need to answer this question when they are in the third or fourth grade. They love you now and they will love you when they are adolescents, but it may not feel like it. Your influence will diminish and shift to their peers somewhere between about eleven and fourteen years of age. You need to place them around other Godly adults who can maintain a balanced mature influence while they go through the normal adolescent transition. A strong youth ministry is like a safety net undergirding what you have been pouring into their lives for the first dozen years.

You may need to get involved with the youth ministry, and providing leadership may be the best option. Your child will be more receptive to this during the middle school transition. My children grew up in a strong youth ministry and I would not have it any other way. You really do not have a choice if it is your desire that they continue to develop spiritually.

My youngest daughter is a sophomore in college and will be going on a vacation this summer with two other girls from two different colleges and an adult lady who is around forty years of age. The relationship between these four began when the girls were about fourteen years of age as this Godly Christian woman in her young thirties at the time began meeting weekly for about an hour with these three girls, often in a coffee shop in our community. The young woman's name is Jennifer Butler. She poured into my daughter's life week by week telling her and the other two girls the same things I would have told them. The exhortation was centered on Bible study and was casual but extremely influential. They are so close and each of the three girls navigated the transitions so very well.

That leads to this idea. Who can you enlist to mentor your child? Is there someone who can supplement what you are seeking to do as a parent? Your child may or may not know you have initiated this but I encourage you to find an adult and/or possibly a student who is a year or two older and of the same gender as your child. Place your child in the pathway of other adults who are willing to invest time with them so that when they are not hearing you as clearly, they are continuing to hear God through others.

How do you leverage influences to help your child navigate the transitions with their spiritual values intact? While there are no guarantees, if you place your child in a strong youth ministry environment where they have long term relationships with other Godly adults in addition to yourself, and if you can get them connected specifically to a mentor, whether it is a vocational pastor or a Godly adult who spends time with them over a period of months if not years, your child will face the same challenges as all others but is much more likely to get through the transitions with a growing faith that carries them into their adult lives. If you can add to that a personal relationship with the senior pastor and quick spiritual connections following the post-high school transition, you will know you did all you could to leverage influences to reinforce what you did as a parent to disciple your child.

QUESTIONS FOR DISCUSSION

1. Which of the transitions described were the most challenging for you?
2. Which of the transitions are facing your child(ren) next?
3. Who mentored you when you were a teen? Who is mentoring you now? Have you ever mentored teens who are not your own children? Could you? Who?
4. Discuss ideas to help with each of the three transitions teens face.

CHAPTER TWENTY-FIVE

STICKY COMMITMENT

Tom Crites

"What a great Father's Day!" I said to myself as I scanned the booth at my favorite restaurant, ready to enjoy my steak. To my right was my lovely wife, Cyndy, smiling as usual listening to the kids' stories of their past week's adventures. My son, Brice, sat across the table with my daughter, Kaylynn, both in their twenties, yet still giggling like they always did at each other's stories and inside family jokes. "Buzz, buzz, buzz...." I tried to ignore the phone vibrating across the table. Quickly, Kaylynn picked up the phone and typed something into the device. "Bing-bong," another phone chimed to alert my son that he had a message. He quickly grabbed the phone, grinned, and in a moment sent a message back to the waiting person on the other end. Feeling the shimmy of my side of the booth, I glanced over to see my wife liking a photo of my nephews. "Wait a minute!" I thought to myself, "Was this day not Father's Day, and am I not the father?" The selfish thoughts heated my blood to simmering. Another "buzz, buzz, buzz..." another "bing bong," and another "buzz, buzz, buzz..." My blood had reached the boiling point as I watched my family engage unseen peers in conversation while their father, on Father's Day mind you, sat in silent obscurity. I was just about to open my mouth to command the phones be put away and for all attention be placed upon me when... "buzz, buzz, buzz." My shirt pocket vibrated. I instinctively took out my phone to see a message: "You have exceeded your monthly data allowance." My daughter coyly stated, "Happy Father's Day... we went over on the data." I could do nothing but smile and drop my head, laughing at the irony of her words and the moment.

Do you remember the good ol' days, when people did not go over their internet data limits!? Yeah, the "good ol' days" were pretty boring. A person had to chat face to face about the weather or describe the details of another day at the office. Now, one can post a selfie, like a cat video, or comment on a witty tweet. Times are so much more interesting... not! It may be because of my age, or because of my introverted personality, but I just do not like being plugged in all the time. I do not want to air all of my business on the internet. I get nervous when people follow me. I need me time, alone time, where I can think and dream. Today's young adults do not have alone time. They are always plugged in. The first thing they do in the morning and the last thing they do at night are to check the messages on their phones. They are in constant contact with their circle of friends, fans, and followers. They live in a state of community. I am not surprised that the third grouped factor we discovered was related to this fact. We found that a young adult was more likely to stay in church if they valued a personal commitment to a spiritual community. Look at the variables that clustered around this factor.

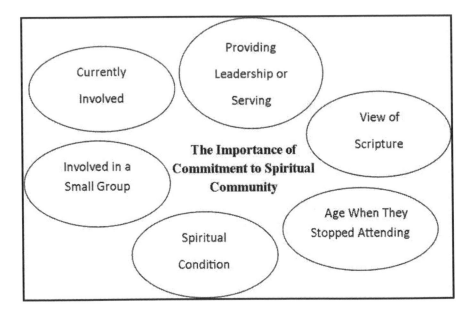

- Are you currently active in the life of a local church? The young adults more likely to stay in church were more likely to be currently active in church and tended to have a high level of church-related activity growing up. While the term "active" could mean different things to different people, I would generally consider an active person as one who at least regularly attends church worship services. Scott Thumma and Warren Bird have split church attendees into two basic categories: spectators and active participants.[36] Their research revealed that the active members are engaged in mission and ministry. They point to a step beyond simple attendance–a place where a person is contributing to the fulfillment of the mission of the church. Yet, I have seen recent definitions of "active" membership refer to attendance or participation in events. Young adults may feel "active" by participating through attendance *and* other ways. Considering the other variables in this factor may shed some light on what a young adult means when he says he is "active" or involved in the church.

- Are you currently providing leadership and/or serving in a local church? This helps us understand that a person is more likely to stay in church when he/she has become more than just the attendee. Here, young adults reveal that those who stay in church tend to have a deeper level of participation beyond simply attending an event. They have demonstrated that they value the spiritual community and look to make their contribution. The Barna group found similar results in their research. They stated that Millennials who remain active in church are twice as likely as dropouts to say they had found a cause or issue at church that motivated them.[37] In this cluster of variables, we saw that as young adults gave themselves through leadership in the church, they were more likely to stay in the church.

- Are you currently involved in a small group Bible study on a regular basis? Young adults value the type of relationships that are developed in a small group. The fact that the small group is focused on spiritual growth is important. Relationships forged in the context of a small group dedicated to the edification of fellow believers make a huge difference in the life of those who stay in church. Barna again has a bit to add to support this: "Those who stay (in church) are twice as likely to have had a close personal friendship with an adult inside the church... The same pattern is evident among more intentional relationships such as mentoring—nearly three in ten active Millennials had an adult mentor at the church other than their pastor, compared to the just one in ten dropouts who would say the same."[38]

- Which would best describe your spiritual state at this time? Young adults who said they are "committed to grow in their faith" or that they currently had a "vibrant faith" were more likely to stay in church than those who indicated that they "lacked commitment." As a matter of fact, we found that young adults were twice as likely to identify themselves as vibrant or committed to grow if they were staying in church. This may be both a cause and an effect of the cluster—the importance of a personal commitment to a spiritual community.

- Thinking about your past church attendance, when did you stop attending church regularly? This variable is critical to understanding how a young adult values the church. Those who stayed in the church longer valued the church more. They had the chance to experience the close spiritual community. Think about this: some kids grow up in church and never experience a close spiritual community. Maybe they attend services regularly, or attend service and Sunday School in obedience to their parents' wishes, but they are not experiencing community. When they leave home for college, military, work, or whatever, they have not had an experience that they valued. Now, in a context where they are able to decide how they spend their time, church does not make their list of important things in life. Barna found that people who are active in church are nearly four times more likely to say they "better understand my purpose in life through church" than those who have become inactive.[39] Those who stayed have found that the church applies to life, and "means something" to them personally. All five of the variables discussed may point to the likely lynchpin in this cluster of variables.

- Which *best* characterizes your view of Scripture? Barna found that: "Millennials who retain a longer-lasting faith than their peers are more likely to find a sense of authority in the Word of God. (Those) who remain active are more likely than those who dropped out to say they believe Jesus speaks to them personally in a way that is real and relevant. Additionally, active church attenders are much more likely to believe the Bible contains wisdom for living a meaningful life."[40] We found the same to be true. In our study, 30% of those more likely to stray from church indicated that they had doubts about the Bible being God's Word, or that it is not reliable (as compared to 2% of those who stayed in church). 98% of those who are more likely to stay in church believe the Bible is very important to believers and should guide them in all they do. Those who are staying in church see the importance of the church. They have found that it is essential for their growth as a person.

A Word for Pastors

Preach the Word! Do not be shy about what the Bible has to say about life. Your congregation is starving for answers to life's challenges. God has given the answers in His Word. Pray that you will be faithful to deliver the bread every week. Remember, you will be called to give an account of your leadership one day. I pray that you will be able to stand and say that you led your sheep to value and love God's Word rather than doubt it or consider it irrelevant.

A Word for Parents

Do not assume that your child, who attends church with you every Sunday, is making important connections in a spiritual community. They may be physically present in a class or group but be totally disconnected. Take time to consider the community that your child is experiencing at church. Is he or she just going through the motions to avoid a conflict with you? Are they spiritually connecting with other kids at church? Are they connecting with other adults who can be good role models? If the answer is no, then you need to investigate how you might encourage them to make the connections. Seek to initiate connections that may grow into important relationships later. Remember that these relationships may be with people outside your church. You may have to seek the help of a coach, community leader, or minister at another church. Make every effort to utilize the moments you have with your child to emphasize the importance of a commitment to a spiritual community. It may be the reason that they stay.

QUESTIONS FOR DISCUSSION

1. How has your church encouraged the spiritual communities that young people need?
2. What are some practical things that a parent can do to encourage a child to make spiritual connections?
3. How can your church help young people become leaders in the church?

CHAPTER TWENTY-SIX

CONNECTING THE DOTS

Tom Crites

In the sixth grade, I had a great language arts teacher, Mrs. Phipps. She loved to read us short mystery stories designed to get us to think about the details. She would dramatically read the tale while we intently listened. I would close my eyes to help process the story, trying to visualize the clues as the story unfolded. However, it was not because I loved mysteries but because I wanted to beat Tracy. Tracy was this very smart girl in my class. She would always solve the mystery. It got on my nerves. After reading the story, Mrs. Phipps would ask the class to solve the mystery, and my hand would shoot up. Even if I did not know, I would take a guess just to beat Tracy. I was usually wrong. After one or two of the class members would take a stab at the solution, Tracy would raise her hand, confident that she had the solution. And she usually did. She had a knack of putting the pieces together to see the big picture. In spite of all my efforts, I almost never saw the solution until after the reveal. I can tell you this, though, I had my fill of mysteries after the sixth grade.

While this book does not reveal a mystery, it does offer pieces to a bigger picture. Parents and pastors can gather the information provided in these pages and apply them to a personal context that may help with their big picture. It is no mystery that we want our children to experience similar blessings that we have enjoyed. Here are three of the clusters identified, using the factor analysis, that seemed to make a difference in a particular situation with regard to those more likely to stay in church. While these three did not carry the same weight as the previous three groupings discussed, they may make a difference in your specific context.

The Importance of Stable Parental Relationships–The research revealed a group of variables related to young adults' family stability. If you remember reading Chapter Twelve, young adults who experienced their parents' divorce were more likely to stray than those who did not face that challenge. However, an interesting dynamic appeared in this grouping. If a young person's parents were divorced, having a strong relationship with both the mother and the father helped to influence them to stay in church. This is encouragement to parents who have a divorce in their past. If they can maintain a close relationship with their children, they may be able to compensate by applying this factor. For example, it does your child no good for you to continuously run your ex through the ringer in front of your kids. Unfortunately, children are thrust into the middle of the conflict. It is unfair for them to be expected or encouraged to "pick sides." For the sake of their spiritual health, avoid spouting off, blowing up, or melting down about their mother or father in their presence. Young adults who were kids of divorce (there were many in our study) shared that if they could maintain a good relationship with their mother *and* their father, no matter the custody issues, they were more likely to stay in church than those who had a good relationship with their mother *or* their father, but not both. So, if you have been through a divorce, try to give your child the space to continue a good relationship with their other parent.

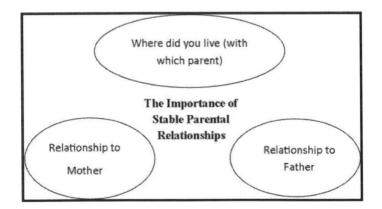

The Importance of Parental Discretion after a Church Crisis–I have heard too many stories of lives devastated by the failures of pastors. I have watched in wonder as church schisms are formed over the most insignificant issues of a church, like the color of the paint or the tempo of the music. The disastrous part of this issue is that 44% of those we surveyed had experienced a church crisis and 25% remembered having a pastor who had a moral failure. Those numbers sadden me. It hurts to know that children had their faith rocked by the sins of those who were to be spiritual examples. Interestingly, the percentages of those more likely to stay compared to those more likely to stray are not significantly different. This tells me there is another dynamic at work to offset the damage that a church crisis can cause.

I believe, true to an important theme in this book, that parents are the key to limiting the damage of a major church crisis. Parents, when crisis erupts in a church body, protect your kids. Shield them from some of the issues that could damage their faith. There may be meetings or discussions that you need to have while they are absent. Consider this: a child may closely relate the pastor to God in their early spiritual formation. If a child were to hear hurtful words about the pastor, or experience an angry outburst aimed toward him or by him, it may taint his understanding of God. A prudent parent will choose the appropriate time and the appropriate information to share with a child concerning the crisis. You will certainly want to leverage any influence you have at your church to be a peacemaker and to seek to help the congregation avert or minimize disputes when possible.

The Importance of Age-Appropriate Discipleship after Conversion–This interesting factor appeared as a variable clustered around the age of conversion, age of baptism, and the theological leanings of the churches where the young adults in our survey grew up. Taken separately, one could be misled to believe that certain faith traditions influence young adults to stay more than other faith traditions, but I do not believe that is what our research shows. The variables in this group clustered in an interesting way. The factor indicated that the older a person was at the time of conversion, combined with a more conservative leaning church, combined with a baptism which occurred close to the conversion, resulted in a person who was more likely to stay. I think the issue that underlies this group is discipleship. Consider the flip side to this factor: a person who was young to very young at the time of conversion, combined with a baptism that occurred before conversion (such as an infant baptism), combined with a more moderate to liberal leaning church was less likely to stay than stray. In this case, if the person is taught, and can understand, the basics of the faith through a system of age-appropriate and biblically faithful discipleship, then they may be more secure in their faith and it may be less likely to fade. I have seen everything from new believer's classes, confirmation classes, basic training retreats, and much more used as effective tools to inform and encourage new believers. There are two important things to consider as a parent and as a minister considering materials and methods for discipleship of new believers. First, consider the age-appropriateness of the materials used. Developmentally, some children may not be ready to understand some of the abstract nature of the faith, and so different materials should be used than those used by older children and youth. Second, consider the religious background of the new believer. Those who have grown up in church will have more of an advanced vocabulary and field of experience to draw upon than a new convert who has little or no church experience.

QUESTIONS FOR DISCUSSION

1. What are some practical things a church can do to encourage the faith of the children of divorced parents?
2. Have you ever known someone who went through a church crisis and seemed to have lost his or her faith? How might the church encourage him/her?
3. What methods are currently used in your church to disciple new believers?
4. What changes should your church consider to help the discipleship of new believers be more age-appropriate and faith background sensitive?

CHAPTER TWENTY-SEVEN

DON'T IGNORE ME

Steve Parr

I busted it! The other day, I went to sit down in a chair at a game table that we have set up in a recreation room in our home. You must know that I am six foot one and weigh approximately a lot. The chair is the type that will swivel 360 degrees and will recline back or rock if it is not in the locked position. I discovered quickly that it was not locked as my momentum overtook the center of gravity over which the middle of the chair was stationed. The shifting weight of my 200-plus pounds moved me swiftly into the recline position and did not stop as the balance was shifted and back I went until I was lying on the floor. Fortunately I was laughing and no injury occurred. I realized quickly that the chair definitely has a tipping point. Lesson learned.

Is there a tipping point for the faith commitment of teens that will propel them into their adult lives with a maturing faith that will last? Here is what you need to understand. Nothing you or I do will guarantee that our children or the students in our church will still be involved as they move into their adult lives. However, you will find that if "A, B, C, and D" are true in the adolescent experience, it is almost certain that they will remain faithful; and if "A, B, C, and D" are not true then they are likely to drop out of church. What are "A, B, C, and D"? Those letters represent the fifteen findings that the chapters in section two are based on. The more that the fifteen issues are true, the higher the likelihood they will stay in church and vice versa. But that is not all. We discovered ten other issues that made somewhat of a difference. The impact was not as great but it was notable, and when you add more to the weight of the momentum of a developing faith, the likelihood that church commitment and faith will stay strong increases.

None of the following issues will make the difference in and of themselves, although any could be used as a source to help propel the faith of the children over which you have influence. Since the research did reveal, however, that each of these issues makes a difference, you would do well not to ignore them. Further, utilize each of the points to add greater weight to the momentum of faith development and drive those you care about to the tipping point and beyond. Instead of a chapter, I will simply devote a paragraph to each of these ten issues and acknowledge on the front end that there may be some mild redundancies, but that should only serve to reinforce some key points. Here we go...

Regular church attendance was balanced. The survey consisted of young adults who grew up attending church, so the fact that they attended has already been established. But how many hours did they spend in church weekly and did it make any difference? The sweet spot proved to be an average of three to four hours in church-related activities each week including a combination of worship, Bible study, service, and social activities. As the hours grew fewer or greater for the respondents, there was a small margin of increased likelihood of having strayed from church as adults. Regular participation was noted, but like the classic story of the *Three Little Bears,* you do not want too much or too little, but to find the amount of time that is just right. Commitment connected with balance is the takeaway I gleaned from this finding.

Growing up with a high view of Scripture. You may recall from the fifteen major takeaways that those still in church tend strongly to have a high view of Scripture. To be clear, those who remained in church tended to believe that the Bible is the Word of God and is reliable, applicable, and trustworthy, having been inspired by God. The high view of Scripture is most often rooted in a family and church that held to a high view and passed that along to their children and teens. The view of parents and the church on the reliability and sufficiency of Scripture as God's inspired Word to mankind tended to point to whether their children were still in church as adults.

Dad was involved in church. You learned earlier that mom and dad serving in the church made a huge difference in the likelihood that the children were in church as adults. What if the dad did not serve? Interestingly, it still made a difference if the father was involved even when he did not serve. Here is another way to view this. If the father is not involved the chances that the children will be in church as adults is much less likely. If he attends church regularly, the children are somewhat more likely to be in church compared to those whose fathers did not attend. However, if dad served in the church, the probabilities go way up. Moms and dads both make a difference and this point drives it home again.

Rotating pastors and youth pastors not allowed. The research revealed that having a series of youth pastors throughout the teen years is more detrimental than not having one at all. Students do tend to look up to those who are called vocationally to serve in this role, and those who bring that calling ordinarily come with skill and passion. However, when youth pastors come and go every couple of years, trust is more difficult to establish, relationships are fractured by the shifts, and teens tend to immunize themselves from the influence of the leaders to insulate themselves from being hurt by another departure. It is understandable that a youth pastor who comes on board will eventually leave. However, when it happens to a teen every couple of years the data showed that those students were less likely to have stayed in church as adults. Likewise, going through several pastors while growing up proved to be detrimental. You may recall that "loving their pastor while growing up" was a major influence on those who stayed in church.

A strong children's ministry. An adult who recalled their church as having a strong children's ministry increased the likelihood of continuing attendance as an adult. While the research showed the value of integrating children with their parents as part of the weekly worship experience, it also elevated the value of targeted ministry opportunities focused on the unique needs of boys and girls. Sunday School, Vacation Bible School, children's choirs, missions organizations, social activities, and special classes focused on children can make a difference if done well. The blend of these activities as well as the names (your church may not call its Bible study "Sunday School") will vary but the principle is the same. Also keep two other things in mind. When asking why adults were still in church, the response, "for my children," was the seventh highest self-described reason. Interestingly, "I have kids" was the seventh most common self-described reason for those who no longer attended. Could it be because the church has no quality ministry for their children? In any case, it is important for each church to provide quality ministry for children and preschool boys and girls.

A strong youth ministry. An adult who grew up attending church who reflected that their experience as a teen included a strong youth ministry was more likely to have stayed in church than one who described the ministry they experienced as weak or non-existent. Remember that more attention is required of one who is immature. It is true with children. A baby requires constant attention and the degree of focus decreases as the child grows until they move on as young adults. The principle is even true with adults. The more immature an adult, the more attention they require. Whether you utilize a volunteer or a vocational minister, the needs of adolescents are so different than any other life stage that it does require specialized attention. Do not neglect to invest in the youth ministry of your church to help it to be strong and influential. The youth ministry, or lack thereof, does influence lifetime commitment.

Attending Christian camps as a teenager. Your church can have a healthy youth ministry whether or not summer camps are part of the equation. However, the research did reveal the value of youth camps for teens. A slight positive correlation was observed between those who attended summer youth camps (Christian-oriented) and the likelihood of continued commitment into young adult life, and it appeared that the more camps attended the better. As a former youth pastor who led hundreds of students on these experiences, I can attest to their value. We would get students away from the pressures of culture for a week in an effort to feed their spirit and they would essentially starve the flesh in contrast with feeding the flesh and starving the spirit as often happens in the weekly life of a teen. Lifelong commitments were begun, breakthroughs were experienced, relationships were deepened, and life changes were made. Interestingly, a slight negative correlation was observed between attending children's camps prior to sixth grade and church attendance as adults. Though the trend was slight, it is worthy of discussion if your church has week long camps for younger children. I do not have an interpretation of that but I did want to report the fact that was discovered.

The influence of peers when growing up. The previous two factors serve as a good segue to this point of emphasis. You no doubt understand the concept of peer pressure and peer influence. People tend to become like those who they spend time with. The research did show that the three or four closest friends one had when growing up had some influence over whether one was still in church as an adult. The principle affirms the reality of peer influence, but since it was a smaller factor should also serve as an encouragement to parents in that their influence is even greater. It may not seem like it at times during the adolescent years. Although Christian teens are by no means perfect, and even though we can all point to "church-going teens" that are bad influences, the reality is that a Christian teen connection is more likely to help propel them to lifetime commitment than a lack of strong Christian friendships. A strong youth ministry and youth camps are a part of the equation.

Changing schools due to multiple moves. You may want to interpret this point in relation to the former in its analysis. A teen that grew up in one community was more likely to still be in church as an adult than one who moved when they were a teen. You know how difficult it is to be in middle school or high school and have to move. Sometimes it is unavoidable and the correlation was slight, yet notable. Interestingly, those who moved a lot were not affected. Perhaps children of military or missionary families learn to adapt compared to that teen who experiences what would be in their view a traumatic move. You may not have a choice, but if you do, take this into consideration if your children are teenagers. If you must move, focus on tipping the scales in a positive direction by applying as many of the other principles as possible to their lives.

The type of community where one grows up. The survey participants were asked if they grew up in the country, in the city, or somewhere in between. To be more specific, the options were very rural, rural, suburban/rural, suburban/urban, or urban. Those who grew up in urban areas or very rural areas were somewhat more likely to have strayed as adults compared to those who grew up in the areas in between. While this may not affect where you live, it may inform the type of community that you choose should you ever find a move necessary. Remember that the goal is to use those things you have influence over to tip the balance toward a greater likelihood of lifetime involvement.

QUESTIONS FOR DISCUSSION

1. Which of the ten issues in this chapter surprises you the most? Why?
2. Of these ten issues, which do you have the most influence over?
3. What patterns do you observe between these ten lesser issues and the fifteen greater issues from Section II?

CHAPTER TWENTY-EIGHT

WHO'S RESPONSIBLE?

Steve Parr

I wept like a baby. That has not happened often in my adult life. I can count on one hand the number of times that I have done anything more than tear up. It happened while I was writing this book. My middle daughter and my son-in-law arrived for Valentines weekend and wasted no time in giving us a card that announced that our first grandchild was on the way. Everyone present was rightfully jubilant. I hugged my daughter, embraced her older sister, and then dismissed myself to my room. Several emotions converged on me in that moment. I experienced joy in knowing that I will be a grandfather, I experienced pain in empathy for my oldest daughter who desires to bear a child but has not yet been blessed, and I experienced praise and an answer to prayer from asking God to grant me the opportunity to see my grandchildren someday. The prayer was prompted to a large degree by the reality that both my father and his father died very young from heart issues.

On top of all of that, I am writing a book about touching this current younger generation desiring that they would come to faith and that those who grow up in church would remain faithful. My burden has increased during this process. While more Christians are alive right now than at any time in the history of the world, how is it that the number of Christians committed to the church in North America is eroding during my lifetime? Who is responsible for this exodus?

Take a moment and allow God to speak to your heart from Psalm 78:1-8.

Give ear, O my people, to my law;
Incline your ears to the words of my mouth.
I will open my mouth in a parable;
I will utter dark sayings of old,
Which we have heard and known,
And our fathers have told us.
We will not hide them from their children,
Telling to the generation to come the praises of the LORD,
And His strength and His wonderful works that He has done.
For He established a testimony in Jacob,
And appointed a law in Israel,
Which He commanded our fathers,
That they should make them known to their children;
That the generation to come might know them,
The children who would be born,
That they may arise and declare them to their children,
That they may set their hope in God,
And not forget the works of God,
But keep His commandments;
And may not be like their fathers,
A stubborn and rebellious generation,
A generation that did not set its heart aright,
And whose spirit was not faithful to God. (NKJV)

What were those "sayings of old" that the Psalmist referenced early in this text? You may recall how the Hebrews experienced a miraculous delivery from bondage when God used Moses to bring the people out of Egypt following 400 years of slavery. God established a testimony of faithfulness all the way back to the life of Jacob and beyond. He established His laws for the nation of Israel. But what about the generations that were not present to experience God's power in such a dramatic fashion? The psalmist is reminding the reader to share the story of God's deliverance faithfully with their children lest they forget what God has done for their nation.

You see in verse seven the consequence of failure to pass

along the story when you reverse the three thoughts. If the next generations fail to hear and embrace these stories as testimonies to God's faithfulness they will not set their hope in God, they will forget the works of God, and they will not keep His commandments. Does that sound familiar? Therefore, according to verse four, the reader should not fail to tell the story to their children. The responsibility extends to the children of the community who may not be hearing the story of God's deliverance from their own parents. Believers are to share the story with the next generation so that the children who are yet to be born will tell the story to their children who are yet to be born.

The text speaks to generational responsibility. I once preached a message with this outline from Psalm 78:

1. The stories we are loving (of our salvation and deliverance from bondage to sin).
2. The students we are losing (sharing statistics of the eroding numbers).
3. The solutions we are learning (similar to much we have discussed in this study).

Who is responsible? I am. You are. For those who have read the text in Psalm 78 and to a lesser degree, for those who have read this book, we have work to do. We are responsible for the next generation. Let us hear them. Let us love them. Let us tell them the story of God's love and grace. Let us not be a stubborn or rebellious generation who failed our children and grandchildren. Start from where you are and commit yourself to God as an instrument to touch a young generation so that they will in turn reach the next generation for Christ. It is time to take responsibility.

QUESTIONS FOR DISCUSSION

1. What does the Bible teach about your responsibility for the next generation?
2. What can you do at your particular life stage to make a greater difference for the faith of the next generation?

PART FOUR
IN THEIR OWN WORDS

CHAPTER TWENTY-NINE

HE SAID, SHE SAID

"*I have stayed because my parents were incredible role models and were actively involved and involved me in their ministry at a young age.*"

"*I have stayed because I found a church that helped guide me through inner healing and brought clarity to my past. I also encountered the Father's heart, the one depicted in the story of the prodigal son.*"

"*I have strayed because I am single in my late thirties and there are no churches that minister to people in my circumstance. I don't really have much in common with the married couples with children of my age group. I also work on Sundays and that makes it difficult.*"

"*I have strayed because I can't find a church that I'm comfortable in. They are either too big and theatrical, too small and gossipy, too granola and hippy, or too straight laced. I live in the suburbs, am married with two children, and still can't find a comfortable place to go, so I just gave up. I have my faith, but it's not an outward, everyday sort of thing. It's something I believe in and follow and I still pray, but I'm just not actively involved in anything.*"

What do you think of those comments? You may or may not agree with what people say but it is important that we hear what they are saying. The research concluded with two open-ended questions where the respondents were allowed to share in their own words why they believed they had remained active in church into their adult lives or why they had dropped out. Over 90% took time to share a response. We took the comments and categorized them so that you could get a quick glimpse of the responses in order to identify patterns. You may in turn determine adjustments or improvements that could be made to your leadership, parenting, or church ministry that might help counter the likelihood that someone will stray.

Before we move to those final two chapters where you will get a sample of the comments and a summary of the responses, there is something you need to know that you can begin to respond to immediately. In our survey, of those who grew up in church but strayed, 39% stated that they intended to get back into the church. That is encouraging. The application has to do with when they intend to return. Almost four in ten said that when they have children they plan to reconnect with the church. What is your church doing to identify expecting parents and parents of preschoolers who are not in church? Almost 40% have a desire to get plugged back in. But you must understand that it is not always easy to go back once you have left for a season of time. It is awkward for some young adults to find their way back into active service. How can you help them? What is your plan? We all have work to do because getting them reconnected is critical if we desire that their children and their children's children will be serving Jesus Christ when they are adults and we are long gone.

CHAPTER THIRTY

I AM NO LONGER ACTIVE
IN CHURCH BECAUSE...

The following are the top ten self-described reasons for straying based on the concluding open-ended question, with a few sample comments made by the respondents.

1. I had a bad church experience.

"I have had a lot of bad experiences with the church. I was called gay by leadership even though I am not and was told I was going to hell because I have tattoos. I was asked to stop serving because some people did not approve of my long hair and tattoos. I have faced a great deal of judgement and a huge lack of honesty in the church which has really put me off. My wife and I started going to another church but I am not active because I have become very guarded. My past experiences left me with a lot of questions as to what is real in Christianity."

"We have been hurt by the church. We are tired of the bureaucracy and the inauthentic faith we see. We are still hopeful to find a 'real' one though."

2. I have intellectual doubts/conflict/Atheism.

"I am struggling with the scientific facts that go against the Bible that are causing me to doubt my faith."

"I would say my lack of faith in the Bible. I can't accept that God can somehow allow man to write plans for his followers. The Christian faith teaches that we are all fundamentally flawed and that through baptism and other acts of penance we can be absolved of sins. Isn't it a logical claim that the men who dictate faith are just as flawed and maybe should not be accepted on faith?"

3. I have relocated and have not found a church.

"I recently moved and have not found a new church yet."

"We are not currently active because we moved and my husband has not wanted to get involved since the move. I did for almost a year, while helping with junior high kids, but he was not comfortable so we switched churches and have rarely gone or gotten connected. I am kind of waiting on him to take the lead."

4. I cannot find a good church.

"I have found that most churches today are treated more like theatrical events more concerned with the 'show' rather than personal growth and this has led to a fake God experience that I don't want to have any part of. I have no desire to attend a church experience and hear about building projects when they can't fill the ones they have got. I hate to be so cynical but want to be honest for the fulfillment of the survey. Thanks."

194

"I cannot find a church that I can connect with or that is welcoming."

5. It conflicts with my work.

"My work schedule hinders me."

"I am usually working during the times of the services."

6. My own fault/struggles/issues/too busy.

"I struggle with the idea of attending alone and to find the motivation on a weekly basis."

"I have had issues that I have let come between me and God. I would feel hypocritical going to church right now."

7. I have children and it is too difficult.

"I have a bad excuse but my three young kids make it hard to serve and be active right now."

"I recently got married and we had a baby. My wife and I were in the process of finding a church together when we decided to pause while our son is an infant."

8. I feel stronger on my own. It is not necessary.

"I feel my faith is stronger when I do it on my own."

"I practice my faith in my own way and speak with friends and family on the topic. Too many churches have split or gone through big changes while I was attending."

9. I am actively looking and just have not yet connected.

"I have not found a church in my college town that I have connected with. I still go to church there but I am not active in it. I really want to find a church to be active in though, but I just haven't found one in the community that I am looking for coupled with solid theology."

"My family is in the process of finding a new church home. We moved to our current town three years ago but recently left the church we initially joined because we have no close connections with any of the members there. We taught a college/career group for a year but made no close friends during the three years we attended. The church was very closed to members who did not fit their mold."

10. Personal apathy and admitted laziness.

"I am not active because upon becoming an adult, I realized that it was no longer 'required' of me to go to church. Apathy set in and soon I became a regular non-attender, though at the time I still believed the overall doctrine. As more time passed and I failed to attend, a more worldly view crept into my mind and many of the things I had accepted as truth for my whole life started to feel distant and unbelievable. Now as a thirty-four year old I honestly do not know what I believe and have no sense of urgency to find out which is related to the aforementioned apathy."

"I am not active because I have been lazy in getting back involved in church. It is my own fault as the leader of my household and I plan on fixing that."

CHAPTER THIRTY-ONE

I AM STILL ACTIVE IN CHURCH BECAUSE...

The following are the top ten self-described reasons for staying based on the concluding open-ended question, with a few sample comments made by the respondents.

1. **Because of my family upbringing.**

   "My parent's faith was just as real in the home as it was outside of it. We never missed a Sunday even when we were on vacation so I felt compelled to find a church when I went to college."

   "I saw my parents taking their Christian faith seriously and through the grace of God surrounded myself primarily with other believers."

2. **I am currently serving and feel obligated.**

   "I serve on the finance team, play occasionally in the band, and I am very involved in a small group that meets every Sunday morning."

   "I have a heart to serve and surround myself with believers. I want my child to see the value of serving others."

3. The grace of God.

"God poured out His love, grace, mercy, and forgiveness upon me."

"I am active because of the grace of God in spite of the failures of people in my life. When I was nineteen the Holy Spirit began dealing with my heart and brought me to the end of myself and Jesus Christ saved me."

4. My faith and love of God and Jesus Christ.

"I love Christ and His church. Serving the community is important to me."

"The Lord saved me and brought me to repentance. He gave me faith in the Lord Jesus Christ and a new heart."

5. It is a priority and I am personally committed.

"My faith in Christ became very vibrant and personal during college when I chose to follow Jesus on my own initiative. My church and small group experience really challenged me to grow. I had a good basis of biblical teaching as a child, but unfortunately did not have sound doctrinal training, especially concerning baptism and Scripture prior to college. Mission trips in college really bolstered my faith as well."

"The Lord has taught me that being part of a church is integral to my growth. It has become a personal decision rather than something I do because it is what I grew up doing."

6. I had a healthy church experience growing up.

"I am active because a youth pastor discipled me when I was a teen."

"My parents were very legalistic, but I found a place that I fit in our church and youth group. I never felt as if I fit in as a teenager but the student ministry gave me a safe place to grow and be myself."

7. For the sake of my children.

"It's very important that my children grow up in church."

"I want my daughter to know that we love the Lord and serve him daily in our community."

8. My faith developed when I was young.

"I am still active because of the influence and example of youth leaders when I was in High School. They encouraged us to grow in our faith and to actively serve in the church even as teens. I had a difficult time fitting in a church during college. The two churches I tried had weak ministries for college age students. After graduating college, I switched back to a smaller church and got plugged back in by being involved in a small group as well as leading a communion set-up team and serving in the children's ministry."

"I developed a strong personal relationship with God when I was younger and had lots of good spiritual influences all throughout my life."

9. I love and need the church.

"Fellowship and accountability among believers is important in my spiritual journey. Other believers challenge me and encourage me to be more like Jesus. Attending church helps fill me up so that I can serve others."

"I've learned that the church is Christ's bride and He loves the church. If He loves it then so should I. The church is my place to serve, learn and a launching place for missions."

10. I have had strong influences and relationships.

"Church has always been part of my life and I enjoy the relationships that I have made in my current church. I have several struggles in my faith but to me church is like a favorite blanket or stuffed animal. I feel safe, loved and welcome in church."

"Brothers stronger in faith came alongside and walked with me."

Do you want to hear more of what they said? To see all of the comments of both those who strayed and those who stayed, visit whytheystay.com or steveparr.net. Our journey has come to an end but the work has just begun. Please begin to apply what you have learned as a parent and as a church leader and share what you have learned with others. We have been honored to share what we have learned and our prayer is that your faith has been strengthened, your heart has been challenged, your skills have been enhanced, and that lives will be changed as we serve the Lord Jesus Christ together. We are so glad that you "stayed!"

ACKNOWLEDGEMENTS

Perhaps you have heard that "life is a team sport," and so it has been with the production of this book. We have worked together from concept to research to analysis to writing. We are just getting started because the message and the lessons from this research are so dynamic and life-impacting. The team effort began with us but extends into many directions

We must begin with our families. Behind every successful man stands a surprised woman, and both of us are blessed with supportive and often surprised wives. We cannot do what we do without their support. Thanks so much to Carolyn Parr and Cyndy Crites for helping both of us to do our best. We both have great children who you have met through our stories. We love them and thank them for letting us tell much of the story through their experiences. Leah Manning, Lauren Martin, and Larissa Parr belong to Steve, along with sons-in-law Greg Manning and Tyler Martin. Kaylynn Crites and Brice Crites belong to Tom.

A special thanks to Lauren Martin and Eddy Oliver for the primary editing along with Stephanie Crites for pre-reading and adding additional feedback. Thanks to Kris Hall for assisting with editing and production. We appreciate Dr. Alvin Reid, Dr. Jeff Iorg, Josh Hunt, Dr. Allan Jackson, Dr. J. Robert White, Pastor Andy Childs, Dr. Greg Abercrombie, Frances Fields, and Gray Morgan for prescreening and providing comments.

We are thankful for the excellent staff at Westbow Publishing. They have been a blessing to us and God is using the staff to touch many lives through publishing excellent Christian books and resources. They are a blessing to leaders who desire to maximize their influence for the cause of Christ.

Most of all, we are thankful to God for His blessings and provision. It is only by His grace and power that we can accomplish anything at all. It is ultimately to His glory that we present this book and our lives.

Steve R. Parr and Tom Crites

ABOUT THE AUTHORS

Dr. Steve Parr serves the Georgia Baptist Convention as the Vice-President of Staff Coordination and Development. In thirty years of ministry he has assisted hundreds of churches in strengthening their ministries by motivating and training leaders through seminars, conferences, preaching, and personal consultations. Steve has a Master of Divinity Degree in Christian Education from New Orleans Baptist Theological Seminary and a Doctor of Ministry degree in Church Growth and Evangelism from The Southern Baptist Theological Seminary. He was featured on the twentieth anniversary of the Billy Graham School of Evangelism of Southern Seminary as one of twenty alumni making a Great Commission impact around the world in 2014.

Steve is a best-selling author of five books including *The Coffee Shop That Changed a Church, Sunday School That Really Excels, Sunday School That Really Responds, Sunday School That Really Works, and Evangelistic Effectiveness: Difference Makers in Mindsets and Methods.*

Steve is married to Carolyn and has three adult children, Leah, Lauren, and Larissa, and two sons-in-law. Follow him on twitter @ steverparr, email Steve at sparr@gabaptist.org, and check out his resources and blog on *Maximized Leadership* at www.steveparr.net.

Dr. Tom Crites has served and studied churches for nearly twenty-five years. He has the unique opportunity to study church health through his work as the Research Specialist of the Georgia Baptist Convention. He also is able to remain on the cutting edge of recent developments in church life through his teaching and mentorship at Liberty University. He has his Master of Divinity degree and Doctorate of Education degree in Educational Leadership from Southeastern Baptist Theological Seminary. He has presented research in many scholarly settings and has had his books and research articles read by thousands of prospective ministers across the country. Tom co-wrote *Evangelistic Effectiveness: Difference Makers in Mindsets and Methods* with Steve.

Tom is married to Cyndy and has two adult children, Kaylynn and Brice. Find him on Linked In, Twitter @ltomcrites, and Facebook. Email Tom at tcrites@gabaptist.org. Follow his research on Facebook at GBC Research–Examining Faith & Culture.

RESEARCH METHODOLOGY
Tom Crites

This chapter is for all the people like me who enjoy seeing the guts of a research project. You may not understand everything that is said in this chapter, but we wanted to include it to confirm the reliability of the study.

Determination of Analysis

We wanted to see if there were any significant differences in the attitudes and experiences of young adults who tend to stay involved in church and those who tend to stray from church involvement. We had some hypotheses on the subject but really did not have a pre-defined idea of how many dimensions existed or the structure of the issue. We developed a questionnaire that focused on a wide variety of variables and determined that an exploratory factor analysis would be the first method for reducing the data to a more comprehendible form.

Development of Face Validity of Questionnaire

An expert panel evaluated the instrument used in this project. The panel consisted of four church specialists with extensive experience and background in church ministry related to young adults. Each was briefed concerning the purpose of the study, given a copy of the instrument, and asked to be brutally honest. They offered input and suggested adjustments that were considered and implemented as agreed upon by the researchers.

After the changes were applied to the questionnaire, it was returned to the experts for a second look. They were instructed to read through the questionnaire one more time to ensure that there were no other changes necessary. This process led to face validation of the terminology, definitions, and language.

External Validity and Reliability of the Instrument

The next step in achieving an acceptable level of validity employed a dual group comparative test technique. A group of six young adults served as a test panel to determine ecological and external validity. After taking the questionnaire, the panel offered written and oral recommendations for clarification of terminology. The clarifications were applied and adjustments made to the instrument.

The questionnaire was distributed randomly to participants responding to invitations via social media and email blasts. The researcher determined to test up to fifty young adults to determine reliability of the instrument. After the first twenty responses were returned, the calculations were completed. A Cronbach's alpha test was calculated to examine the internal consistency of the survey. All but one question was included in the analysis due to the open-ended nature of the final question on the questionnaire. For 52 of the 53 questions, a = 0.781, which is considered an acceptable level for reliability.[41] In addition to the Cronbach's alpha test, a Spearman-Brown Coefficient and a Guttman Split-Half Coefficient were used to verify the reliability of the instrument. Both coefficients yielded acceptable results as seen in table 1 and table 2 below.[42]

Table 1: Cronbach's Alpha Reliability Statistics

Cronbach's Alpha	N of Items
.781	52

Table 2: Spearman-Brown Coefficient and
Guttman Split Half Reliability Statistics

Correlation Between Forms		.734
Spearman-Brown Coefficient	Equal Length	.847
	Unequal Length	.847
Guttman Split-Half Coefficient		.782

Based on the findings of Morgan and Gliner[43], the instrument has high levels of validity and reliability.

Steps, Assumptions and Sample

The planned design of this study followed the common factor analysis model. Factor analysis involves the study of order and structure in multivariate data. It includes both theory about the underlying constructs and dynamics which give rise to observed phenomena, and methodology for attempting to reveal those constructs and dynamics from observed data.[44] I followed the four basic steps required to conduct a factor analysis. First, I calculated a correlation matrix of all variables to be used in the analysis—thank you Lord for computers. Second, each factor was assigned an Eigenvalue, identifying the factor with the greatest variance. Eigenvalues are used in this type of analysis to sort the factors by proportion of variance from the greatest to the least. This allows the researcher to select the combination of variables whose shared correlation represents the greatest amount of variance in the study. Then, I had to "rotate" the factors to create a more understandable factor structure. Finally, Steve and I interpreted the results. We identified seven factors or clusters that we needed to evaluate on a deeper level. This process follows the standard acceptable steps for using a factor analysis.[45]

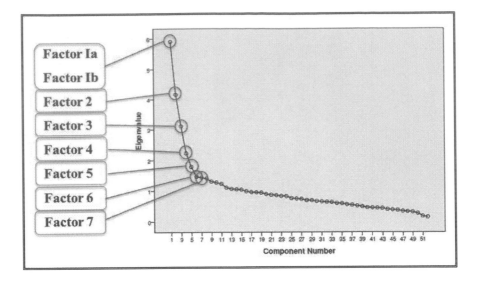

Several assumptions apply to the usage of factor analysis. Garson offers a comprehensive overview of the assumptions connected.[46] We followed his guide to see if the data measured up to the statistical method. Factor analysis lends itself to the confusion of factor labels. To avoid compromising factor labels, our panel of experts was utilized to help select general labels for the imputation process. During this study, we assumed that the cases are similarly related and no outliers exist. Garson warns that outliers—anomalies outside of an expected range of values, can impact correlations heavily and thus distort factor analysis, however I found none. Interval data was assumed. Thus, homoscedasticity, having equal or similar variances, was assumed as well. Orthogonality, statistical independence, was assumed as well, realizing that each factor was a stand-alone contributor to the data. Underlying dimensions shared by clusters of variables are assumed. If this were not the case then the study would not be necessary. You can trust that we did all the necessary tests to make sure that the information that we had and the methods that we wanted to use for analysis were in order.

Our sample size was excellent as we had 1,393 usable questionnaires. This yielded a 99% confidence level with a +/- 3.46 confidence interval for the sample. We were extremely confident that what we discovered represented what young adults were feeling and experiencing. When we split the participants into categories, we continued to have quality samples for comparative purposes. For some of the analysis, a sample of 140 "not currently involved" participants was sectioned off. We continued to have confidence in our study due to the number in that group far exceeding the guidelines in the Central Limit Theorem.[47]

We did several post-hoc t-tests to dig deeper in the variables that were identified in the initial factor analysis. When we evaluated these, we found several to be significant; these were included in the chapters that you just read.

BIBLIOGRAPHY

"5 Ways to Connect with Millennials," *Barna Group*, last modified September 10, 2014, https://www.barna.org/barna-update/ Millennials/682-5-ways-to-connect-with-Millennials#. VNDv9E9oxMs.

Barna, George. "Evangelism is Most Effective Among Kids," *Barna Group*, last modified October 11, 2004, https://www.barna. org/barna-update/article/5-barna-update/196-evangelism-is-most-effective-among-kids#.VJQ5N5CdA.

"Baby Boomers Retire," *Pew Research Center*, last modified December 29, 2010, http://www.pewresearch.org/daily-number/ baby-boomers-retire/.

Career Advisory Board, *The Future of Millennial's Careers*, Career Advisory Board: Downers Grove, IL, 2011.

Carnegie Mellon University "Millennial Segmentation Survey," *Carnegie Mellon University Integrated Innovation Institute*, 2014, accessed January 2, 2015, http://www.cmu.edu/ integrateinnovation/media/Millennials.html.

Christie, Nancy and Michael Gauvreau. eds. *The Sixties and Beyond: DeChristianization in North America and Western Europe, 1945–2000*. Toronto: Toronto University Press. 2012.

"Church Dropouts: How Many Leave Church between Ages 18–22 and Why," *Lifeway Research*, last modified Spring 2007, http://liveabove.com/documents/research/   Part%20 1%20Church%20Dropouts_How%20Many%20Leave%20 Church%20and%20Why.pdf.

Darren, George and Paul Mallery. *SPSS for Windows Step by Step: A Simple Guide and Reference 12.0 Update.* Boston: Pearson Education, 2005

Dobson, James. *Parenting Isn't For Cowards.* Dallas, TX: Word Publishing, 1987.

"Five Trends among the Unchurched," *Barna Group*, last modified October 9, 2014, https://www.barna.org/barna-update/culture/685-five-trends-among-the unchurched#. VWxmU8vbJMs.

Garson, David. "Factor Analysis Overview," accessed September 13, 2014 http://www2.chass.ncsu.edu/garson/pa765/factor.htm

Ham, Ken, Britt Beemer, and Todd Hillard. *Already Gone: Why Your Kids will Quit Church and What You Can Do To Stop It.* Green Forest, AR: Master Books, 2009.

Henry, Matthew. "Commentary on the Whole Bible: Psalms 78," *Bible Study Tools*, accessed January 4, 2015, http://www. biblestudytools.com/commentaries/matthew-henry-complete/psalms/78.html.

Holmes, Thomas H. and Richard H. Rahe. "The Social Readjustment Rating Scale." *Journal of Psychosomatic Research*, accessed February 2, 2015, http://www.edmondschools.-net/Portals/3/docs/Terri_McGill/READ-Adjustment%20 scale.pdf.

Ingram, Chip. *Effective Parenting in a Defective World,* Carol Stream, IL: Tyndale House Publishers, 2006.

Johnstone, Patrick and Jason Mandryk, *Operation World: 21st Century Edition*. Crownhill, Milton Keynes, UK: Paternoster Press, 2001.

Junco, Reynol and Jeanna Mastrodicasa. "Connecting to the Net. Generation: What Higher Education Professionals Need to Know About Today's Students," *National Association of Student Personnel Administrators*, 2007.

Kim, David. *20 and Something: Have the Time of Your Life (and Figure It Out Too)*. Grand Rapids, MI: Zondervan, 2013.

Kinnaman, David. "Most Twentysomethings Put Christianity on the Shelf Following Spiritually Active Teen Years," *Barna Group*, last modified September 11, 2006, https://www.barna.org/barna-update/millennials/147-most-twentysomethings-put-christianity-on-the-shelf-following-spiritually-active-teen-years#.VWxl2cvbJMs.

_____. *You Lost Me: Why Young Americans are Leaving the Church, and Rethinking Faith*. Grand Rapids, MI: Baker Publishing Group, 2011.

Lyons, Gabe and David Kinnaman. *Unchristian: What a New Generation Really Thinks about Christianity and Why It Matters*. Grand Rapids, MI: Baker Books, 2007.

MacArthur, John. *The Fulfilled Family*. Chicago, IL: Moody Press, 1987.

Morgan, George and Jeffrey Gliner. "Helping Students Evaluate the Validity of a Research Study." *American Educational Research Association*, last modified March 24, 1997, http://files.eric.ed.gov/fulltext/ED408349.pdf.

Neuman, Scott. "Millennials' Talk to God' but Fewer Rely on Religion, Survey Finds," *NPR*, last modified 2014, http://www.npr.org/blogs/thetwoway/2014/04/11/301969264/-Millennials-talk-to-god-but-fewer-rely-on-religion-survey-finds.

Nouwen, Henri. *Bread for the Journey, A Daybook of Wisdom and Faith,* New York: Harper One, 2006.

Nunnally, J. C. *Psychometric Theory.* New York: McGraw-Hill Publishers, 1978.

Palfrey, John and Urs Gasser. *Born Digital: Understanding the First Generation of Digital Natives.* New York: Basic Books, 2008.

Powell, Kara and Chap Clark. *Sticky Faith: Everyday Ideas to Build Lasting Faith in Your Kids.* Grand Rapids, MI: Zondervan, 2011.

Rainer, Thom. *The Bridger Generation: America's Second Largest Generation, What They Believe and How to Reach Them.* Nashville, TN: Broadman & Holman, 2006.

Sahlin, Monte and David Roozen. "A Profile of Churches and Other Congregations with Significant Young Adult Participation," *Hartford Seminary,* last modified 2010, http://faithcommunitiestoday.org/profilechurches-and-other-congregationssignificantyoung-adult-participation.

Schroer, William. "Generations X, Y, Z, and the Others" *Social Librarian,* accessed December 11, 2014, http://www.socialmarketing.org/newsletter/features/generation3.htm.

Smith, Christian. *Soul Searching: The Religious and Spiritual Lives of American Teenagers.* New York: Oxford University Press, Inc., 2005.

Thompson, Van. "What Percentage of High School Students Attend college After Graduation?" *The Classroom,* accessed February 3, 2015, http://classroom.synonym.com/ percentage-high-school-students-attend-college-after-graduation-1423.html.

Thumma, Scott and Warren Bird, *The Other 80 Percent: Turning Your Church's Spectators into Active Participants.* San Francisco, CA: Josey-Bass, 2011.

Tucker, Ledyard and Robert MacCallum. *"Exploratory Factor Analysis,"* last modified 1997, http://www.unc.edu/~rcm/book/ch1.pdf.

"U.S. Department of Education Institute of Education Sciences National Center for Education Statistics," *Fast Facts*, last modified 2013. http://nces.ed.gov/fastfacts/display .asp?id=98.

Warner, Rebecca. *Applied Statistics: From Bivariate through Multivariate Techniques*. Thousand Oaks, CA: Sage Publications, 2013.

Zettersten, Rolf. *Dr. Dobson: Turning Hearts Toward Home: The Life and Principles of America's Family Advocate*. Dallas, TX: Word Publishing, 1989.

NOTES

1   Ken Ham, Britt Beemer, and Todd Hillard, *Already Gone: Why Your Kids will Quit Church and What You Can Do To Stop It.* (Green Forest, AR: Master Books, 2009), 22.

2   David Kinnaman, "Most Twentysomethings Put Christianity on the Shelf Following Spiritually Active Teen Years," *Barna Group*, last modified September 11, 2006, https://www.barna.org/barna-update/millennials/147-most-twentysomethings-put-christianity-on-the-shelf-following-spiritually-active-teen-years#.VWxl2cvbJMs.

3   "Five Trends among the Unchurched," *Barna Group*, last modified October 9, 2014, https://www.barna.org/barna-update/culture/685-five-trends-among-the unchurched#.VWxmU8vbJMs.

4   "Church Dropouts: How Many Leave Church between Ages 18–22 and Why," *Lifeway Research*, last modified Spring 2007, http://liveabove.com/documents/research/Part%201%20Church%20Dropouts_How%20Many%20Leave%20Church%20and%20Why.pdf.

5   "Baby Boomers Retire," *Pew Research Center*, last modified December 29, 2010, http://www.pewresearch.org/daily-number/baby-boomers-retire/.

6   Thom Rainer, *The Bridger Generation: America's Second Largest Generation, What They Believe and How to Reach Them.* (Nashville, TN: Broadman & Holman, 2006), 169.

7   David Kinnaman, *You Lost Me: Why Young Americans are Leaving the Church, and Rethinking Faith.* (Grand Rapids, MI: Baker Publishing Group, 2011), 22.

[8]   Ibid, 19.

[9]   Kara Powell and Chap Clark, *Sticky Faith: Everyday Ideas to Build Lasting Faith in Your Kids.* (Grand Rapids, MI: Zondervan, 2011), 15.

[10]   Monte Sahlin and David Roozen, "A Profile of Churches and Other Congregations with Significant Young Adult Participation," *Hartford Seminary*, last modified 2010, http://faithcommunitiestoday.org/ profilechurches-and-other-congregationssignificantyoung-adult-participation.

[11]   Rainer, *The Bridger Generation.*

[12]   Christian Smith, *Soul Searching: The Religious and Spiritual Lives of American Teenagers.* (New York: Oxford University Press, Inc., 2005), 170.

[13]   Gabe Lyons and David Kinnaman, *Unchristian: What a New Generation Really Thinks about Christianity and Why It Matters.* (Grand Rapids, MI: Baker Books, 2007).

[14]   David Kim, *20 and Something: Have the Time of Your Life (and Figure It Out Too).* (Grand Rapids, MI: Zondervan, 2013), 84.

[15]   Nancy Christie and Michael Gauvreau, eds. *The Sixties and Beyond: DeChristianization in North America and Western Europe, 1945–2000.* (Toronto: Toronto University Press. 2012).

[16]   William Schroer, "Generations X, Y, Z, and the Others" *Social Librarian*, accessed December 11, 2014, http://www.socialmarketing. org/newsletter/features/generation3.htm.

[17]   Reynol Junco and Jeanna Mastrodicasa, "Connecting to the Net. Generation: What Higher Education Professionals Need to Know About Today's Students," *National Association of Student Personnel Administrators,* 2007.

[18]   Kinnaman, *You Lost Me.*

[19]   Smith, *Soul Searching.* And Carnegie Mellon University "Millennial Segmentation Survey," *Carnegie Mellon University Integrated Innovation Institute*, 2014, accessed January 2, 2015, http://www. cmu.edu/integrateinnovation/media/Millennials.html.

20 Scott Neuman, "Millennials' Talk to God' but Fewer Rely on Religion, Survey Finds," *NPR*, last modified 2014, http://www.npr.org/blogs/thetwoway/2014/04/11/301969264/-Millennials-talk-to-god-but-fewer-rely-on-religion-survey-finds.

21 Career Advisory Board, *The Future of Millennial's Careers*, (Career Advisory Board: Downers Grove, IL, 2011).

22 John Palfrey and Urs Gasser, *Born Digital: Understanding the First Generation of Digital Natives,* (New York: Basic Books, 2008), 5.

23 Henri Nouwen, *Bread for the Journey, A Daybook of Wisdom and Faith,* (New York: Harper One, 2006), 30.

24 Matthew Henry, "Commentary on the Whole Bible: Psalms 78," *Bible Study Tools*, accessed January 4, 2015, http://www.biblestudytools.com/commentaries/matthew-henry-complete/psalms/78.html.

25 George Barna, "Evangelism is Most Effective Among Kids," *Barna Group*, last modified October 11, 2004, https://www.barna.org/barna-update/article/5-barna-update/196-evangelism-is-most-effective-among-kids#.VJQ5N5CdA.

26 Rolf Zettersten, *Dr. Dobson: Turning Hearts Toward Home: The Life and Principles of America's Family Advocate,* (Dallas, TX, Word Publishing, 1989). A good example is James Dobson, who testifies to a conversion age of three.

27 Chip Ingram, *Effective Parenting in a Defective World*, (Carol Stream, IL: Tyndale House Publishers, 2006).

28 Thomas H. Holmes and Richard H. Rahe, "The Social Readjustment Rating Scale." *Journal of Psychosomatic Research*, accessed February 2, 2015, http://www.edmondschools.-net/Portals/3/docs/Terri_McGill/READ-Adjustment%20scale.pdf.

29 Barna. "Evangelism is Most Effective Among Kids."

30 John MacArthur, *The Fulfilled Family,* (Chicago, ILP: Moody Press, 1987). See particularly chapters 7 and 8.

31 James Dobson, *Parenting Isn't For Cowards,* (Dallas, TX: Word Publishing, 1987), 106.

32 Ibid, see especially chapter 6.

33 Van Thompson, "What Percentage of High School Students Attend college After Graduation?" *The Classroom*, accessed February 3, 2015, http://classroom.synonym.com/ percentage-high-school-students-attend-college-after-graduation-1423.html.

34 "U.S. Department of Education Institute of Education Sciences National Center for Education Statistics," *Fast Facts*, last modified 2013. http://nces.ed.gov/fastfacts/display .asp?id=98.

35 Patrick Johnstone and Jason Mandryk, *Operation World: 21st Century Edition*, (Crownhill, Milton Keynes, UK: Paternoster Press, 2001), 13–14.

36 Scott Thumma and Warren Bird, *The Other 80 Percent: Turning Your Church's Spectators into Active Participants.* (San Francisco, CA: Josey-Bass, 2011).

37 "5 Ways to Connect with Millennials," *Barna Group*, last modified September 10, 2014, https://www.barna.org/barna-update/Millennials/682-5-ways-to-connect-with-Millennials#. VNDv9E9oxMs.

38 Ibid

39 Ibid

40 Ibid

41 J. C. Nunnally, *Psychometric Theory.* (New York: McGraw-Hill Publishers, 1978).

42 Ibid

43 George Morgan and Jeffrey Gliner, "Helping Students Evaluate the Validity of a Research Study." *American Educational Research Association*, last modified March 24, 1997, http://files.eric.ed.gov/fulltext/ED408349.pdf.

44 Ledyard Tucker and Robert MacCallum, "*Exploratory Factor Analysis*," last modified 1997, http://www.unc.edu/~rcm/book/ch1.pdf.

45 Darren George and Paul Mallery, *SPSS for Windows Step by Step: A Simple Guide and Reference 12.0 Update.* (Boston: Pearson Education, 2005).

[46] David Garson, "Factor Analysis Overview," accessed September 13, 2014 http://www2.chass.ncsu.edu/garson/pa765/factor.htm

[47] Rebecca Warner, *Applied Statistics: From Bivariate through Multivariate Techniques* (Thousand Oaks, CA: Sage Publications, 2013).